COMPUTERS: ONE CLICK AT A TIME

A Beginner's Guide for Using Computers with Ease

By Angela Harris

TGX TGX Development
Adult Education

Computers: One Click at a Time

© 2017 TGX Development, LLC

Published by TGX Development, LLC
P.O. Box 14214
Research Triangle Park, NC 27709
E-mail: sales@tgxdevelopment.com
Web Site: www.tgxdevelopment.com

Computers: One Click at a Time
ISBN 978-0-692-95592-5

Bulk Purchase

TGX Development Adult Education publications are available for special premiums and sales promotions as well as for fund-raising use. Book excerpts also can be created to specifications. Additionally, content can be repurposed and licensed for online programs. For details, contact sales@tgxdevelopment.com.

Printed in the United States of America

Computers: One Click at a Time

TABLE OF CONTENTS

About This Book

We're now living in a faster world where technology is changing rapidly every day. In the blink of an eye, there is a new gadget or software application to consider, or a new way to perform a job with more ease. Machines are replacing more and more physical and knowledge-based tasks, and there are no signs that the pace of change will subside.

How do you make sense of computers in a way that's beneficial and puts you in the driver's seat? How do you keep up and not get left behind? How do you protect yourself and your personal information? How do you make informed decisions? How do you use computers to better yourself and your way of living?

This workbook will enable you to answer these questions and calm any fears about computer use. Upon completing this workbook, you will begin the journey of using computers safely and effectively in the home, on the job, and for fun.

What can you find in this book?

- **Objectives** at the beginning of each lesson to frame what you can expect to learn.

- **Key Terms** in every lesson to build your computer vocabulary.

- **Practice Exercises** to reinforce basic computer skills and practical know-how.

- **Answer Keys** allowing you to check your work on activities and keep track of your progress.

LESSON ONE: Using a Computer

Introduction

Objectives – After completing this lesson, you will be able to:

- Describe how the use of a computer solves everyday problems
- Identify common types of computers
- Differentiate between computer parts that are input and output devices
- Explain the importance of speed, memory, and space when using a computer
- Purchase a computer that will meet your needs
- Turn on a computer
- Use a mouse to perform tasks
- Recognize and use the main keys of a keyboard
- Select a printer that will meet your needs

Key Terms

- Computer
- CPU
- Desktop
- Hard Drive
- Hardware
- Inkjet
- Keyboard
- Laptop
- Laser Printer

- Memory
- Monitor
- Mouse
- Refurbished Computer
- Software
- Tablet
- Touchpad
- Wearable Device
- Webcam

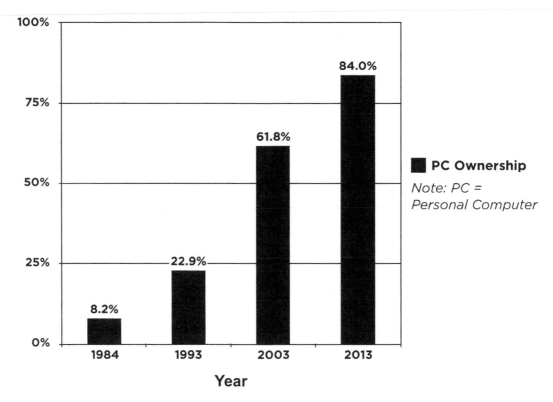

Chart 1: Computer Ownership by American Households (2013)
Source: U.S. Census Bureau

Computers have become a very important part of everyday life. We rely on computers at home, on our jobs, for **leisure** activities, and to communicate with others. Computers have made many tasks easier to perform. By knowing how to use computers, people are able to get things done in a more organized and timely manner. For example, instead of filling out paper job applications and submitting them at a physical location, many job applications can be filled out and submitted online with the click of a mouse.

It's hard to imagine life without computers. Computers come in a variety of shapes and sizes and can be used for many purposes. However, this **widespread** use of computers was not always the case. Up until the late 1970s or early 1980s, computers were mostly used by large corporations and governments. It was rare for the average person to have a computer in their home. In the early 1980s, companies such as Apple and IBM began making computers available for consumers. About three **decades** later, nearly 84 percent of U.S. households could be found with some sort of computer device in the home (see Chart 1).

Activity #1

Directions: It's time to check your understanding of the background of computers. Read each question. Circle the **best** answer.

1. According to Chart 1, what percentage of U.S. households owned a computer in 1993?

   A) 61.8%

   B) 84%

   C) 22.9%

2. Based on the passage, what is meant by the **widespread** use of computers?

   A) Computers can be found in every country in the world.

   B) Computers are used by many different people for a variety of purposes.

   C) Computers are so large that they can cover an entire desk.

3. Leisure can be defined as **free time to do something that you enjoy**. According to the passage, we rely on computers for leisure activities. Which one of the following activities is most likely to be a leisure activity made possible by the use of computers?

   A) writing a resume

   B) cleaning the house

   C) listening to music

4. A decade is a **period of ten years**. Referring to Chart 1, approximately how many decades are between 1984 and 2013?

   A) three

   B) four

   C) two

5. **True** or **False**. Write **T** for True or **F** for False next to the statements below.

   _____ a) In the early 1970s many people began purchasing computers for personal use in the home.

   _____ b) According to Chart 1, computer ownership by American households more than doubled from 1993 to 2003.

The R.E.E.L.

The R.E.E.L.

Real Experiences in Everyday Life

Computers play an important role in everyday life. From writing and sending e-mail to checking a bank account balance online to finding various locations using Google Maps, the computer has become that one machine that is hard to live without. In the "Background" section of this lesson, you learned how computers assist with tasks related to the workplace, home, and leisure activities. It's now time to take a closer look at how computers are used in the real world.

Directions: Look at each picture in the left column. Use the space in the right column to describe briefly how the use of a computer (or a computer program) is solving a problem or making life easier or more enjoyable.

Picture	What role does the computer play?
GPS	
SLOT MACHINE	

Purchasing a Computer

For many people computers are considered a major purchase. With most major purchases, it is important to do the proper research in order to make the best buying decision. However, there are millions of people who think that they are not smart enough to choose the right computer. In this section we will discuss key features of a computer and how you can determine the qualities that are most important to you. But before we begin, can you circle the objects below that are a type of computer?

A **B** **C** **D**

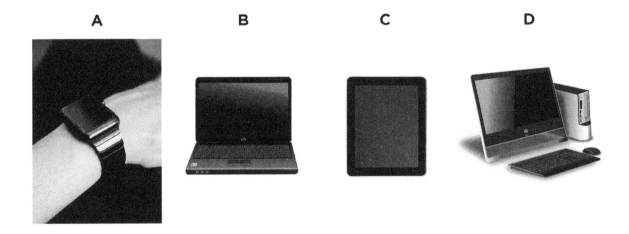

How many items did you circle? Can you identify each device? Write your answers below.

A _____

B _____

C _____

D _____

Why Speed?

- People want a computer that will not take forever to complete the instructions given to it.

- The **CPU**, or central processing unit, processes the instructions it receives from the software and other programs. It is the brain of the computer.

- The CPU is one of the main components that makes a computer fast.

- A computer is faster when it can process more and more information every second.

- A dual processor will be faster than a single processor.

- Higher clock speeds, measured in gigahertz (GHz), means better performance.

- GHz means one billion cycles per second.

- **Tip:** Keep in mind that the faster the CPU, the higher the cost of the computer. Also, your electricity bill is likely to increase from the extra energy and heat that the faster processor creates. Thus, make sure that your CPU is well-balanced with your memory, hard drive space, and graphics card for optimal performance. For example, no need to have a super fast processor and limited memory. In fact, for simple tasks like surfing the Web, sending e-mails, and typing documents, a low-range to mid-range CPU should satisfy your needs.

CPU Manufacturer	Low-End Processor	High-End Processor
Intel	Core i3's	Core i7's
AMD	Athlon 64	Phenon II

Why Memory?

- The **memory** is where the computer stores programs and information while it is using them.

- More memory allows you to run more programs at once.

- Generally, the faster the memory, the faster the speed at which information is processed.

- **Tip:** Consider the type of user you are and make sure the amount of memory meets your needs.

What type of user are you?	Memory Needed
Casual User: Surfing the Web, e-mailing, and listening to music	1GB – 2GB
Everyday User: Surfing the Web, e-mailing, word processing, listening to music, watching videos	2GB – 4GB
Student: Surfing the Web, e-mailing, word processing, photo and video editing, gaming, doing many tasks at once	4GB – 8GB
Professional User/Gamer: High performance gaming, high-definition video, multimedia editing, graphics design, serious multitasking	8GB – 16GB

Why Space?

- Everything you keep on your computer is on a **hard drive**. The hard drive stores your documents, pictures, music, videos, programs, and preferences.
- The size of the hard drive affects how much space is available for programs and personal files.
- Photos and videos often take up a great deal of hard drive space.
- **Tip:** Consider purchasing a computer with 500GB (GB = Gigabyte) or 1TB (TB = Terabyte) of hard drive space, especially if you plan on using several programs during the life of your computer or storing large video files.

SAVINGS ALERT: If you only need a computer for simple tasks like typing documents, surfing the Web, and sending and receiving e-mails, you can save a great deal of cash by purchasing a **refurbished computer**. A refurbished computer is one that a customer returned and cannot be resold as new, or a computer that failed to meet the manufacturer's quality tests and was rebuilt. You can buy one directly online from companies like Dell or Hewlett Packard (HP) or from a small, local reseller like Computer Renaissance (1-888-COMPREN or www.compren.com). Again, do your research and find the solution that is best for you.

What type of computer can you expect to purchase based on your needs?

User Need	Computer Price Range
Casual User: Surfing the Web, e-mailing, and listening to music	budget or refurbished
Everyday User: Surfing the Web, e-mailing, word processing, listening to music, watching videos	budget or refurbished
Student: Surfing the Web, e-mailing, word processing, photo and video editing, gaming, doing many tasks at once	mid-range to high-end
Professional User/Gamer: High performance gaming, high-definition video, multimedia editing, graphics design, serious multitasking	mid-range to high-end

Howie's How-Tos on Purchasing a Computer

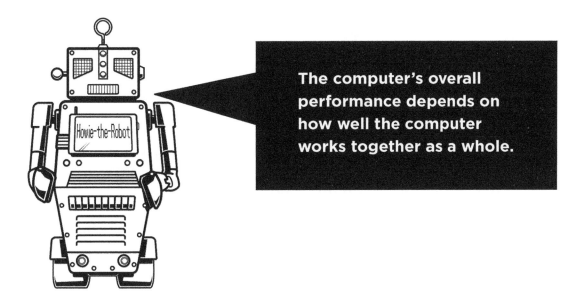

The computer's overall performance depends on how well the computer works together as a whole.

To summarize, here's a recap from Howie-the-Robot on how to purchase a computer.

1) Consider <u>what</u> you want to do, <u>where</u> you want to do it, and <u>how much</u> you're prepared to spend.

2) Buy the most computer, in terms of features, that you can afford.

3) Do your research.

4) Shop around for the best deal.

Activity #2

Directions: Your job is to help Pam, Sergio, Robert, and Selina purchase a computer. They each have different needs and want a computer that will fit their lifestyle. Read each description of the different types of computers. Then, read the comments made by Pam, Sergio, Robert, and Selina and use these comments to select the best computer that will fit their needs.

Desktop: This type of computer is meant to be set up in one location and left there for a long period of time. Parts include a tower, monitor, keyboard, and mouse.

Laptop: This type of computer is small and can be carried with you wherever you go.

Tablet: This type of computer is a hand-held device with a touchscreen interface that can be carried with you wherever you go.

Wearable Device: A device that can be worn on the body and generally tracks information related to one's health and fitness.

Computer Buyer	Comments	Best Computer?
1) Pam	"I need a small device that I can take with me during my morning walks. The device needs to track my number of steps, calories burned, and heart rate."	
2) Sergio	"I need a small computer that I can take with me when I study in the library."	
3) Robert	"I need a computer that I can keep on my desk in my office. It needs to have a wide screen and keys large enough for my big fingers."	
4) Selina	"I need a computer that I can take with me when I travel on vacation. I will mainly use it to read eBooks, so having a touchscreen interface is important to me."	

Activity #3

Directions: It's now time to test your knowledge of computer parts. Take a few moments to review the **hardware** below. Then, select the name from the parts list that best identifies the part and write that name next to the corresponding number in the table. Also, indicate whether the part is an **input** or **output** part, if applicable.

1   2   3   4

5   6   7   8

Parts: Tower   Keyboard   Monitor   Wireless Mouse
              Mouse   Touchpad   Printer   Webcam

	Computer Part	"Input" or "Output"
1		
2		
3		
4		
5		
6		
7		
8		

Activity #4

Directions: Now that you can identify the main parts of a computer, it's important to understand what each part does. Draw a line to match the computer part with the best description. Feel free to refer to the pictures in Activity #3 if you need help.

Computer Part	Description
Tower	When given instructions to do so, this output device will place words and images on paper.
Mouse	We can use this input device to type words, numbers, and symbols.
Keyboard	We click the buttons on this input device to make choices and give the computer information. No wire is needed.
Touchpad	This part is generally placed on the floor and contains smaller parts of a desktop computer.
Monitor	This input device can be used to see and talk to family and friends around the world. It can also be used to make videos.
Printer	We click the buttons on this input device to make choices and give the computer information.
Wireless Mouse	This input device is generally used instead of a mouse when using a laptop and requires movements by one's fingers.
Webcam	This output device presents information from the computer on the screen.

Turning on the Computer

Windows Start Symbol   *Power Button*

Turning on the computer is quite easy. It requires that you press the power button. Most computers have a power button that looks like a circle with a small opening at the top and a short, vertical line in the middle. Some people think of the symbol as the letters "I" and "O." Many computers will have an LED light that keeps the symbol lit while the computer remains on.

What happens when you want to turn your computer off?

When you are ready to turn your computer off, you should avoid pressing the power button. If you turn the computer off using the power button, you run the risk of losing your data. Even though you may have finished using your computer and closed all of your programs, the computer could still be performing "invisible" operations. These "invisible" operations include saving your settings, sending data, and receiving data. You can damage or lose data by stopping these important actions mid-stream. Thus, the best way to turn off your computer is to go to the start button located on your screen and select "shut down," "hibernate," or "sleep." These options refer to computers that run the Windows operating system, which we will cover in further detail in Lesson Three. The "shut down" function will also vary based on the version of the Windows operating system that you are using.

Hibernate mode will save your open documents and completely turn off your computer, using zero power.

Sleep mode, on the other hand, allows you to save your open sessions and return to them later while the computer enters a low-power state.

Directions: Read each question. Circle the **best** answer.

1. Circle the image that best represents the power button on a computer.

2. Based on the passage, what is the best way to turn off your computer?

    A) Press the power button

    B) Unplug the computer's power supply

    C) Go to the start button located on your screen and select "shut down," "hibernate," or "sleep"

3. **True** or **False**. Write **T** for True or **F** for False next to the statements below.

    _____ a) In sleep mode, the computer is not completely turned off.

    _____ b) In hibernate mode you can return to your open sessions later.

Using a Mouse

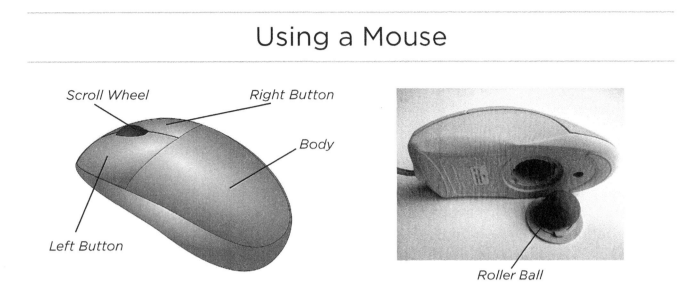

Scroll Wheel   Right Button

Body

Left Button

Roller Ball

For some computer users, learning to use the mouse in the right way takes some practice. Generally speaking, a typical mouse has three main parts: the body, left and right buttons, and a little button shaped like a wheel in the center. The button in the center is called a **scroll wheel**. The body of the mouse has a roller ball or laser that tracks the movement of the mouse. When you move the mouse on your desk or mouse pad, the roller ball or laser will move your pointer, also called the **cursor**, on the computer screen in the same direction that you move the mouse. If you lift your mouse up in the air, you will not be able to move your cursor on your screen. Thus, it is important to keep your mouse on a flat surface with the front end of the buttons pointing towards the computer screen.

The best way to hold a mouse is based on individual user preference. However, many people rest their hand over the body of the mouse with their index finger on the left button, their middle finger on the right button, and their thumb on the side. Most mice are designed for right-handed people. Individuals who are left-handed can use their middle finger to press the left button or set up their mouse in a way that will work best with their left hand. It is also possible to purchase a customized mouse made specifically for people who are left-handed. Many computer and office supply stores will typically carry a left-handed mouse.

Pressing either the left or right mouse button will help you navigate through programs and menus on your computer. When you press either button, you will hear a soft clicking sound. For most simple tasks, you will use the left mouse button and will click either once or twice. A single click will allow you to select items and move items by dragging and dropping them. This drag and drop motion entails clicking and holding the left button as you move, or **drag**, the mouse, until you are ready to release, or **drop**, the item that you are moving. Double-clicking is often needed to open a program or file on your computer. Lastly, using the scroll wheel is optional. The scroll wheel enables you to move the page up and down when you are on the Internet or in many software programs.

If you are using the touchpad on a laptop instead of a mouse, you can tap the touchpad with your fingers to get the same clicking effect. A single tap will provide the same reaction as a single click. Likewise, a quick double tap will provide the same effect as double-clicking a mouse.

Keep in mind that the cursor will look differently depending upon where you are on the screen and the type of task that you are performing. Don't be alarmed if you see your cursor change to reflect different images. Each image is the computer's way of communicating to you its status and its readiness to perform the task that you desire. The table below will help you recognize the different changes that your cursor may undergo.

Pointer	**Text Cursor or "I" Bar**	**Hand Pointer**	**Hourglass or Circle**
As you move around and select items on your screen, the cursor will look like an arrow.	Indicates that you can enter text.	Indicates a hyperlink that will link you to another page if you click on it.	Indicates that the computer is waiting for something to load, such as a Web site or program.

Howie's How-Tos on Using a Mouse

Move your mouse slowly for better navigation rather than too fast.

Here are a few tips from Howie-the-Robot on how to use a mouse.

1) Keep your mouse on a level surface.

2) Hold the mouse firmly in place with your thumb and pinkie for better control. This tip will work whether you are right-handed or left-handed.

3) If you're going to be using a computer for long periods of time, consider obtaining a wrist rest to use with your mouse. A wrist rest can limit hand fatigue and unnecessary injury to the hand and wrist.

Using a Keyboard

Figure 1-1: Keyboard Keys

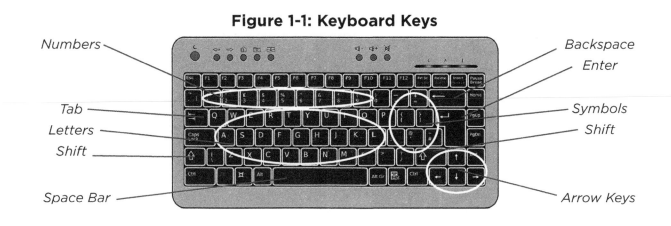

As discussed earlier, a keyboard is an input device that allows you to type words, numbers, and symbols into the computer. A keyboard has individual keys that provide specific instructions. Some keys are letters, some are numbers, some are symbols, and others help you choose where and how to type.

The letter keys are located in the center of the keyboard. The number keys run across the top of the keyboard and are also on the right of the keyboard. The symbol keys include the question mark, period, and comma. These keys can be found to the right of the letter keys. Keys such as *Enter*, *Shift*, *Caps Lock*, *Backspace*, *Space Bar*, *Tab*, and *arrow keys*, surround the letters, numbers, and symbols keys. Becoming familiar with the location and function of these keys can help you use a computer more effectively.

In **Figure 1-1**, the *Shift* key looks like an arrow pointing upward. Pressing the Shift button will allow you to type capital letters and the symbols that are at the top of the number keys. A *Shift* key can be found on the left and right side of the keyboard. Letting go of the *Shift* key will enable you to type lower case letters and numbers again. If you want to type a series of capital letters, pressing the *Caps Lock* button once will allow you to do so without having to hold down the *Shift* key while you type. Simply press the *Caps Lock* button again to turn it off.

When you make a mistake, both the *Backspace* and *Delete* buttons will allow you to erase your mistake. The *Space* bar lets you put a space between words while the *Tab* key puts a bigger space between words (about five spaces). The *Enter* key moves your cursor down a line, and the *arrow keys* will move your cursor in all directions, one line at a time, on the page or screen – up, down, left, and right. Use the *Home* key to take you to the beginning of the line and the *End* key to jump to the end of the line. The *Page Up* (*PgUp*) and *Page Down* (*PgDn*) keys will allow you to move multiple lines at a time up and down the page or screen.

Activity #6

Directions: Consider each task below numbered one (1) through ten (10). Refer to the list of ten keyboard keys and write the name of the key that would <u>best</u> accomplish the task listed in the left column of the table.

Enter	Delete	Tab	Space Bar	Caps Lock
Shift	Home	Page Up	Backspace	End

Task	Keyboard Key
1) Put a space between words or letters	
2) Erase the letter to the right of the cursor	
3) Capitalize the first letter of a person's name	
4) Move the cursor down to the next line	
5) Put five spaces at the beginning of a paragraph	
6) Move to the beginning of the line	
7) Move up the screen several lines at a time	
8) Remove a sentence that you just typed by moving backwards	
9) Capitalize an entire sentence for emphasis	
10) Go to the end of the line	

Selecting a Printer

Choosing a printer starts with identifying your needs. Will you be printing mostly black-and-white text or color pictures? How quickly do you want to be able to print documents? Will your computer be strictly for home use or for both home and work tasks? What is your budget?

Once you understand your printing needs, you can make a better decision about the type of printer to use. The two most common types of printers for general home use are laser printers and inkjets. A laser printer uses a laser beam, drum, heat, and pressure to place toner, which is a dry powder type of ink, onto a sheet of paper in the form of text and images. An inkjet printer sprays very fine drops of ink on a sheet of paper to create text and images. In the past, the cost of laser printers was considerably more than the cost of an inkjet. Now, however, introductory models can be acquired at relatively the same cost. Below are strengths and weaknesses of each type of printer.

Laser Printer Strengths:

- **Speed** – prints pages more quickly than an inkjet printer
- **Low cost** – toner cartridges cost less over time
- **High-quality text** – black text and line graphics are more crisp compared to an inkjet printer
- **Great for large jobs** – capable of handling high-volume print jobs

Laser Printer Weaknesses:

- **Warm-up time needed**
- **Slightly higher upfront costs**
- **Paper limitations** – heat-sensitive papers or materials cannot be used for printing

Inkjet Strengths:

- **Easy availability**
- **Low start-up cost** – most inkjets tend to be less expensive than laser printers
- **High-quality images** – great for photos and image-heavy documents
- **Paper variety** – ability to print on many types of paper, including glossy photo paper, textured stationery, and fabrics
- **Re-usability** – inkjet cartridges can be refilled and reused

Inkjet Weaknesses:

- **Expensive ink**
- **Ink smearing** – inkjet ink is water-based and can fade and smear easily
- **Slowness** – prints pages much slower than a laser printer

The R.E.E.L.

Real Experiences in Everyday Life

Which printer would you choose for the following workloads? Circle your answer.

- Family photos   inkjet or laser printer

- Heavy volumes of   inkjet or laser printer
  text-based documents

- Small school projects   inkjet or laser printer

Key Terms

Computer	A type of machine that can follow stored instructions.
CPU (Central Processing Unit)	The brains of the computer responsible for processing the instructions received from software and other programs.
Desktop	A type of computer that is meant to be set up in one location and left there for a long period of time.
Hard Drive	Hardware that stores documents, pictures, music, videos, programs, and user preferences.
Hardware	All the parts of a computer system that can be physically touched.
Inkjet	A type of printer that sprays very fine drops of ink on a sheet of paper to create text and images.
Keyboard	An input device used to type words, numbers, and symbols on the computer.
Laptop	A small computer that can be carried and used on the go.
Laser Printer	A type of printer that uses a laser beam, drum, heat, and pressure to place toner, which is a dry powder type of ink, onto a sheet of paper in the form of text and images.

Key Terms

Memory
The computer's storage area that holds data and instructions.

Monitor
An output device that presents information from the computer on the screen.

Mouse
An input device that allows a user to make choices and give the computer information by clicking.

Refurbished Computer
A computer that a customer returned and cannot be resold as new, or a computer that failed to meet the manufacturer's quality tests and was rebuilt.

Software
Programs that tell a computer exactly what to do.

Tablet
A small hand-held computer with a touchscreen interface.

Touchpad
An input device that can be used instead of a mouse when using a laptop. It requires movements by one's fingers to communicate instructions.

Wearable Device
A computer that can be worn on the body and generally tracks information related to one's health and fitness.

Webcam
An input device that allows users to see and talk to family and friends.

Introduction

Objectives – After completing this lesson, you will be able to:

- Recognize common desktop icons
- Quickly access open programs using the task bar
- Access information in the notification area
- Use the scroll bar and helpful buttons to manage windows

Key Terms

- Bookmark
- Desktop
- Icon
- Scroll Bar
- Taskbar
- Title Bar
- Web Browser

The Desktop

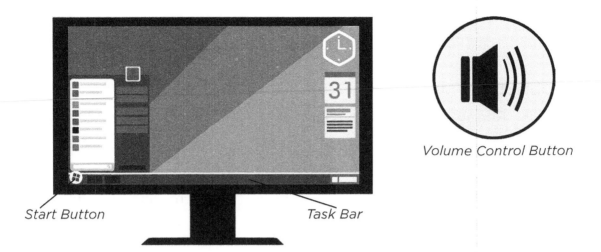

Volume Control Button

Start Button   Task Bar

The **desktop** is the first screen that you see when you turn on your computer. Depending on the version of Microsoft Windows you are using, you will see a start button and a horizontal taskbar at the bottom of the screen.

The **taskbar** contains open programs and may also include popular programs that you use often. When you have multiple windows open on your computer screen, it is convenient to refer to the taskbar in order to access quickly the program that you want to use. The taskbar also includes a notification area to the far right that displays information such as the time, date, and volume control. Clicking on the volume control button allows you to adjust the sound. Most computers allow you to move the button up and down and mute the sound. Additionally, you may be able to see your Internet connection status to determine whether your computer is connected to the Internet.

The desktop may also present small pictures or logos. These small images are called **icons** and generally represent a software program, document, folder, Web browser, or Internet location. Double-clicking on an icon will open, or launch, the software program.

A **Web browser** is a software application that provides access to the Internet and allows you to view Web pages on your computer. Popular Web browsers include Mozilla Firefox, Google Chrome, Microsoft Edge (formerly Internet Explorer), and Apple Safari (if using a MacIntosh computer made by Apple Inc. or another manufacturer using Apple's operating system). Most Web browsers allow you to save your favorite Web pages as a **bookmark** or **favorite**.

Bookmarks, also called favorites, are simply saved shortcuts that direct your browser to your favorite locations on the Web. Creating a bookmark entails adding the bookmark, or favorite, to your bookmarks menu. Once the bookmark is added, you can click the bookmark instead of typing the entire Web address when trying to locate your favorite Web pages. Additional information on using Web browsers can be found in Lesson Four.

We will discuss the operating system in more detail in Lesson Three. Generally, the operating system can be defined as a program that manages the hardware and other software on the computer. Most personal computers employ the Microsoft Windows operating system.

Activity #1

Directions: It's time to assess your familiarity with the computer desktop. Carefully review the computer screen below. Each letter represents a specific area of the computer. Read each question and circle the **best** answer based on the information in the passage about "The Desktop."

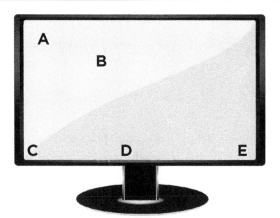

1. Where would you find the start button?

    A) area A

    B) area B

    C) area C

    D) area D

2. Where would you find the taskbar?

    A) area A

    B) area B

    C) area C

    D) area D

3. Where would you find the notification area?

    A) area A

    B) area B

    C) area C

    D) area E

4. Where would you find desktop icons?

    A) area A

    B) area B

    C) areas A and B

    D) area C

5. Where would you find the volume control?

    A) areas A and B

    B) area C

    C) areas D

    D) area E

Managing Windows

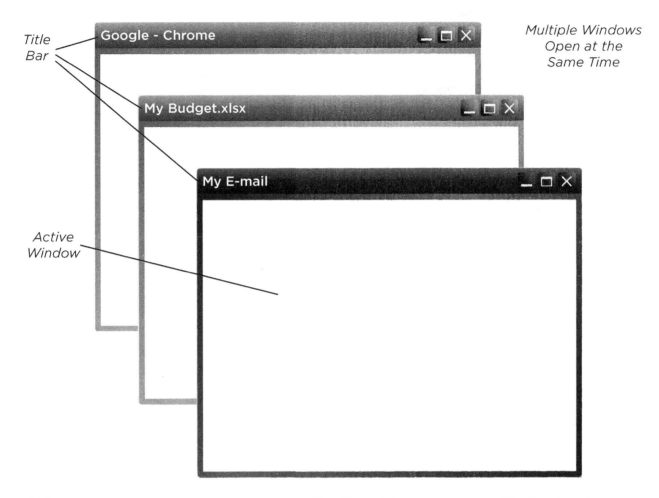

Title Bar

Active Window

Google - Chrome

Multiple Windows Open at the Same Time

My Budget.xlsx

My E-mail

When you open a program or application, the program will display in a new window. At the top of the window will be a **title bar**, which shows the name of the folder, document, or program. You can have multiple windows open at the same time. For example, you could be entering numbers into a spreadsheet for a budget in Microsoft Excel while doing research online using Google Chrome as your Web browser. You might also have another window open that presents your electronic mailbox, allowing you to respond quickly to incoming e-mail messages. The **active window** will have a highlighted title bar and will appear in front of the other windows.

Windows help you to perform various tasks at once in an organized manner. Additionally, each window that you open will be shown as a button on the taskbar at the bottom of the screen. The active window button on the taskbar will be a different color. If you want to access a certain window immediately, you can point your mouse over the button on the taskbar and select the application that you want to see on your computer screen.

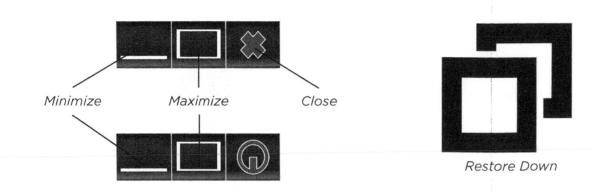

Minimize   Maximize   Close

Restore Down

Managing windows is a little easier with the use of three helpful buttons that can be found in the upper right hand corner of each window. The **minimize button** looks like an underline or an underscore. If you want to remove a window from your screen temporarily, click on the minimize button. Minimizing a window will enable you to open other applications while preventing your screen from appearing too crowded. The window you removed can be accessed from the taskbar when you are ready to use the application again. The **maximize button** allows you to bring a window to the full screen size. When your window is in full screen mode and you want to return to the small screen size, you will notice that the maximize button has changed to the **restore down button**. Clicking on the restore down button will change the size of the window back to its original, smaller size.

The third button that will enable you to manage windows more effectively is the **close button**. It looks like a big X. The close button will close an application along with its corresponding window. If you are working in a program like Microsoft Word and have made changes to your document, you will be prompted to save your changes before the window closes. If you choose not to save your changes, any unsaved data that you entered will be lost. Thus, it is always a good idea to periodically save your work, particularly when using multiple applications at the same time.

Scroll Bar

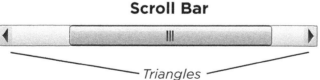

Triangles

Another nice feature to help navigate the information that appears in a window is the scroll bar. The **scroll bar** allows you to move around the window so that you can fully view a document, program, Web page, or other information that will not fit on one screen. Clicking on the small triangle at each end of the scroll bar will allow you to move left and right or up and down, depending on whether you use the scroll bar that is on the right hand side of the window or the scroll bar that is at the bottom of the window. With a little bit of practice, you will be able to manage the windows on your screen thoughtlessly.

Activity #2

Directions: Read each question. Provide the **best** answer(s).

1. Which button allows you to hide a window?

    A) restore down

    B) minimize

    C) maximize

2. Which button allows you to make a window larger and fill the screen?

    A) close

    B) maximize

    C) restore down

3. Which bar shows the name of the folder, document, or program that you are using?

    A) taskbar

    B) scroll bar

    C) title bar

4. Provide at least two (2) ways that you will know that a program that is open on your computer screen is active and ready for your use.

    1) _____

    2) _____

5. Based on what you have learned thus far in the first two lessons of this book, identify four ways that you can move up and down a Web page that is too large to fit on one screen.

    1) _____

    2) _____

    3) _____

    4) _____

Key Terms

Bookmark A saved shortcut that directs your Web browser to your favorite locations on the Web.

Desktop The first screen that you see when you turn on your computer.

Icon Small pictures or logos appearing on a desktop that represent a software program, file, or folder.

Scroll Bar A useful feature of a window that permits movement up and down and from side to side when there is a document, program, Web page, or other information that will not fit on one screen.

Taskbar A bar at the bottom of the computer screen that contains the start button, a notification area, open programs, and other applications that are used often.

Title Bar The bar at the top of a window that shows the name of the folder, document, or program that is being used.

Web Browser A software application that provides access to the Internet and allows Web pages to be viewed on the computer screen.

LESSON THREE: Software

Introduction

Objectives – After completing this lesson, you will be able to:

- Identify popular operating systems used for different devices
- Recognize the advantages of word processing software
- Describe commonly used word processing icons
- Manage simple data using a spreadsheet
- Perform basic math calculations using spreadsheet formulas
- Apply shortcut keys to save time in Excel
- Protect your computer with anti-virus software

Key Terms

- Android
- Anti-Virus Software
- Chromebook
- Chrome OS
- Firewall
- Font
- Interface
- iOS
- Linux
- Malware
- Open-Source
- Operating System
- Ransomware
- Spreadsheet
- Spyware
- Template
- Tizen
- Virus
- Word Processing

The Operating System

macOS

Microsoft Windows

Linux

In Lesson Two we defined the **operating system** as a program that manages the hardware and software on a computer. When you purchase a computer, the manufacturer will pre-load the operating system. The most popular operating systems for personal computers are Microsoft Windows, macOS, and Linux. Microsoft Windows, or Windows, is an operating environment developed by Microsoft that organizes information and provides a graphical interface that helps the user complete tasks in an easy-to-use fashion. An **interface** allows the exchange of information among the hardware, software, humans, and the input and output devices connected to the computer.

The macOS family presents a graphical interface created by Apple for its Macintosh line of personal computers. The latest release from the macOS family features a desktop interface with three-dimensional appearance characteristics. Instead of seeing just the width and height of images and text, users are also able to perceive the depth, or length.

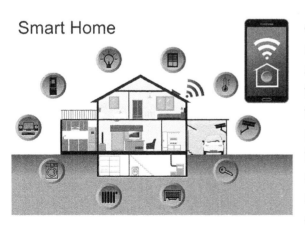

Smart Home

Linux (pronounced LINN-ux) is a family of **open-source** operating systems. An open-source operating system is freely available and can be modified by anyone around the world. Many computer appliances in the home are powered by Linux, as Linux provides a low cost operating system solution for manufacturers. Examples of these smart appliances include refrigerators, thermostats, and laundry appliances that operate using a computer chip.

Two other lesser known operating systems that deserve mention are Chrome OS and Tizen. **Chrome OS** is designed by Google and is also considered an open-source system. It uses the Google Chrome Web browser as its user interface and mostly supports Web applications. Chrome OS can be found running on **Chromebooks**, which are small laptops designed to be used while connected to the Internet. **Tizen** is another open source system. It is used primarily in smart appliances, wearable devices, in-car entertainment systems, televisions, and virtual reality headsets made by Samsung.

Activity #1

Directions: Read each question and provide the **best** answer(s).

1. If you were to purchase an HP (Hewlett Packard) desktop, which operating system would you expect to find running on your machine?

    A) Chrome OS

    B) Microsoft Windows

    C) macOS

    D) Linux

    E) Tizen

2. If you were to purchase a MacBook Pro, which operating system would you expect to find running on your machine?

    A) Chrome OS

    B) Microsoft Windows

    C) macOS

    D) Linux

    E) Tizen

3. If you were to purchase a Lenovo ThinkPad, which operating system would you expect to find running on your machine?

    A) Chrome OS

    B) Microsoft Windows

    C) macOS

    D) Linux

    E) Tizen

4. If you were to purchase a Samsung smart TV, which operating system would you expect to find running on your television?

        A) Chrome OS

        B) Microsoft Windows

        C) macOS

        D) Linux

        E) Tizen

5. The "Smart Home" image below presents icons of several items in a smart home that could be powered by an operating system. Can you list five of these items?

SMART HOME

1) _____

2) _____

3) _____

4) _____

5) _____

6. Referring back to Question #5 and the "Smart Home" illustration, what other "smart" items might be found in the home that are not represented in the image? Name at least two.

1) _____

2) _____

7. Street cameras are often used by police and law enforcement agencies to improve roadway safety while capturing important information that saves time and money and possibly simplifies an internal process. Many street cameras employ a state of the art operating system that allows many value-added applications to occur. Look at the picture of the street cameras below. Read the list of applications. For each application, suggest a problem that is being solved.

Street Cameras

Application   **What problem is being solved?**

1) Cameras track when and where
    a vehicle enters and exits a toll road.   _____

2) Cameras measure a vehicle's speed.   _____

3) In a parking lot, cameras store the
    license plate of vehicles along with
    the parking ticket number.   _____

4) Cameras monitor the vehicles coming
    to and leaving a major sporting event.   _____

5) Cameras identify hazardous goods
    being transported through a tunnel.   _____

The R.E.E.L.

Mobile devices run on operating systems that are developed specifically for mobile devices. Google Android and Apple iOS are two well-known operating systems that run on mobile devices. Google maintains the **Android** mobile operating system and gives it away for free to makers of mobile devices. **iOS** is the mobile operating system designed by Apple to run on its line of mobile devices.

Can you tell which mobile operating system is running each mobile device below? (Hint: For the two smartphones, look at how each phone is designed and determine the manufacturer.)

_____

_____

_____

Word Processing

Word processing is the creation, editing, and formatting of text using computer software. Many workplaces demand a general knowledge of word processing software. Even at-home users find word processing a useful tool for creating documents and accomplishing household duties. Most word processing programs enable tasks such as drafting letters, creating to-do lists, and writing papers. With additional skill it is also possible to change fonts, align text, insert tables, and check spelling. A **font** is a representation of text in a stylistic way. Some fonts are simple while others can be fancy, cursive, or mimic a typewriter font. Fonts can vary based on design, point size, weight, and color. The table below highlights some safe fonts that tend to work well when using either Windows or macOS.

Safe Fonts

Arial	Comic Sans
Georgia	**Impact**
Trebuchet	Verdana

Becoming familiar with a word processing program will help you create documents that are attractive and readable. You can set margins, change line spacing, develop headers and footers, and use the thesaurus to improve word choice for an overall professional presentation. Microsoft Word for Windows and Pages for Mac are two commonly used word processing programs. However, there are other options with similar features comparable to these programs. Google Docs and Writer, for example, are two applications that are rated highly by users and critics alike. Google Docs is a free online application that supports multiple users of the same document and provides editing and document storage. Writer, which is part of the WPS Office suite software, is a free word processing application that is compatible with Microsoft Word and can be used with many different operating systems.

Activity #2

Directions: You have just been given a document to format using Microsoft Word. However, before you can make the necessary changes to the document in an efficient manner, you must understand the purpose of commonly used word processing symbols. For each icon below, write its purpose. (Hint: Use the pictures to help you, as the purpose is closely related to the look of the icon.)

Icon	Purpose
B	
I	
U	
ABC ✔	
≡	
≡	
≔	
🔍	
↺	
A	

The R.E.E.L.

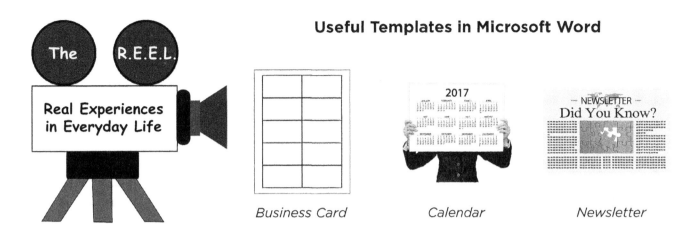

Useful Templates in Microsoft Word

Business Card Calendar Newsletter

A **template** is a sample document that provides a useful layout for completing similar documents. Many software programs include preinstalled templates that make creating documents easy and fast. It is also possible to download templates that are compatible with various software programs. Microsoft Word, for example, includes templates for resumes, cover letters, business cards, calendars, and newsletters. Most templates contain standard text, pictures, and placeholders for you to insert your own information. Referring to the business card template on the left, create the front and back of your very own business card using the template on the right.

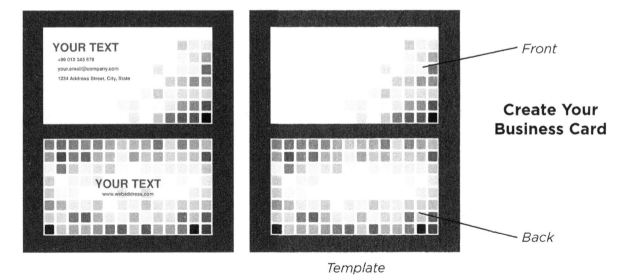

Create Your Business Card

Front

Back

Template

You do not have to own a business to have a business card. In fact, business cards are a great way to share your contact information with others.

Spreadsheets

Figure 3-1: Sample Excel Spreadsheet

	A	B	C	D	E	F
1		Number of Rooms	Bedrooms	Bathrooms	Garage (Y/N)	Office (Y/N)
2	House 1	12	4	3	Y	N
3	House 2	10	4	2	N	N
4	House 3	16	5	4	Y	Y
5	House 4	8	3	2	N	N
6	House 5	7	2	1	N	N
7		*53*				

A **spreadsheet** is a computer application divided into rows and columns that manages data and performs different calculations. Users of various skill levels find spreadsheets helpful, as they offer many advantages over calculators and pencil and paper. One of the most popular spreadsheet programs is Microsoft Excel. Each Excel file consists of a workbook that contains one or more worksheets. The smallest unit in a worksheet is a **cell**, which looks like a rectangular box. Excel names columns using letters and labels rows using numbers. A cell is identified by a column letter and a row number. In **Figure 3-1**, for example, cell D5 has a value of "two" and denotes column D (i.e., the fourth column) and row 5 (i.e., the fifth row). Cell B7 shows the sum of all the rooms included in houses one through five.

One of the key benefits of using Excel and other spreadsheet programs is the ability to do basic math such as addition, subtraction, multiplication, and division. These math calculations are performed by always beginning the formula with an equal sign (=) in the cell. The equal sign can be followed by numbers, a cell identifier (e.g., C2), a mathematical symbol, or a function. The table below highlights commonly used symbols in spreadsheets along with their meaning and an example.

Symbol	Meaning	Example
= (equal sign)	Equal to; starts a formula	= 5*2+7 (cell value will be 17)
+ (plus sign)	Addition	= 4+7 (cell value will be 11)
- (minus sign)	Subtraction	= 10-2 (cell value will be 8)
* (asterisk)	Multiplication	= 3*4 (cell value will be 12)
/ (forward slash)	Division	= 8/2 (cell value will be 4)
% (percent sign)	Percent	10%
^ (caret)	Exponentiation	= 2^3 for 2^3 (cell value will be 8)
: (colon)	Range or series of cells	B3:D3
SUM (function)	Adds values, cell references, ranges, or a mix of all three	= SUM(B2:B6) (referring to **Figure 3-1**, cell value will be 53)

The best way to become familiar with spreadsheets is to practice. With practice, you will see that programs like Microsoft Excel are extremely useful. Once you enter data and create formulas for needed calculations, you can add and delete columns and rows and learn to perform more advanced tasks such as keeping column titles in sight as you scroll and creating graphs. For now, focus on mastering the basics. Also, remember that you can format the appearance of the data you are using (e.g., bold versus italics column labels) and exercise some control over the types of numbers you choose to enter. Instead of working with standard numbers only, you can choose to have your numbers appear as a percentage or currency. You can also set the number of decimal places and add borders and colors to your cells for more emphasis.

Howie's How-Tos on Spreadsheet Shortcuts

Now that you understand simple spreadsheet lingo and how to perform basic calculations, there are faster ways to get work done in a spreadsheet. Here are five (5) of my Tricks of the Trade using shortcut keys.

What do you need to do?	Shortcut Keys
1) Copy highlighted text	**Ctrl+C**
2) Paste highlighted text	**Ctrl+V**
3) Save your work	**Ctrl+S**
4) Open a recent spreadsheet file	**Ctrl+O**
5) Format cells quickly using a preferred format	• Select the cell or cells containing the format you want to copy • Press **Ctrl+C**, which will copy the cell(s) to the Clipboard • Select the cell(s) that you want to receive the format • Press **Alt+E**, **S**, **T**, **Enter**

Activity #3

Directions: Figure 3-2 provides financial information for Candy Café over a six-month period. Review the information and answer the questions that follow, using your knowledge of spreadsheets.

Figure 3-2: Candy Café Financial Information

	A	B	C	D	E	F	G	E
1		January	February	March	April	May	June	Total
2	Sales	$21,000	$22,000	$23,000	$23,500	$24,000	$25,000	**$138,500**
3	Expenses	$20,900	$21,100	$21,900	$22,200	$22,700	$23,100	**$131,900**
4	Profits	$100	$900		$1,300	$1,300	$1,900	
5								

Note: Sales - Expenses = Profits

1. In what cell will you find sales for the month of February? _____

2. In what cell will you find profits for the month of May? _____

3. What month is in cell D1? _____

4. What range of cells represents expenses for January through June? _____

5. Using cell references, write a formula that expresses the value of profits for the month of March. _____

6. How much profit was earned in March? _____

7. Using the SUM function, write a formula to express the value of total sales for January through June. _____

8. Using cell references, write a formula to determine the total profits for January through June. _____

9. Using the value you found in Question #6, what are the total profits for January through June? _____

Antivirus Software

Virus – computer code capable of damaging a system or destroying data.

Malware – a program designed to harm a computer or device. Short for malicious software.

Spyware – a program that can collect and transmit personal information about another's computer activities without the user being aware.

Ransomware – software that prevents access to a computer system until a sum of money is paid.

Antivirus software is designed to shield the computer from harmful attacks by detecting and removing all threats and potential threats. Many people think that antivirus software is unnecessary. However, we live in an age where highly talented individuals are capable of doing massive damage to computer systems through viruses, spyware, malware, ransomware, and other threats. Security professionals agree that antivirus software is a good investment, especially if your computer has sensitive or important information stored on it that you cannot afford to lose.

The good news is that many computers come with a preinstalled antivirus program for a trial period. Once the trial period ends, you have to decide whether to pay a subscription fee or opt for a free program that you can download on your system from the Internet. If you do decide to download a free antivirus program, be sure to choose a familiar Web site. Avast Antivirus, AVG AntiVirus, Malwarebytes, and Microsoft Windows Defender (Microsoft Security Essentials if using an older version of Windows) are four well-known brands with free offerings. Be sure to do your research to weigh the pros and cons of each.

What should you look for in an antivirus program?

- **Malware protection** that shields your computer system from viruses and other threats.

- A **firewall** that prevents malware from downloading and blocks a harmful Web site from grabbing data off your computer.

- **Resource considerations** – Will the program require substantial memory or take a long time to scan your files for threats, draining resources needed for other tasks?

- An **up-to-date version** of the software program so that your antivirus protection will be able to handle the latest attacks and threats.

Optional Features

- **E-mail filter** to block unwelcome e-mails.
- **Child filter** that prevents access to Web sites that are not suitable for children.
- **File backup** to back up your files to another drive periodically.

What can you expect to pay for antivirus software that is not free?

Expect to pay between twenty (20) and sixty (60) dollars for the initial year of service. To renew the service, you will have to pay another forty (40) to eighty (80) dollars per year. Most prices will depend on the features included in the software package. Also, the price that you pay typically includes installation on multiple computers in the same household.

Activity #4

Directions: Read each scenario. Provide the **best** answer.

1. Anna clicked on a link she received via e-mail from what appeared to be a legitimate delivery company. She expected to receive tracking information on a package. Instead, when she clicked on the link, her computer locked and she couldn't type anything using her keyboard. A message appeared demanding that she go to her nearest Wal-Mart and wire $1500 to an unknown recipient in order to be able to use her computer again and have access to her files. What sort of threat is Anna experiencing??

   A) a virus

   B) spyware

   C) ransomware

2. Bobby returned to work after taking a brief lunch break. To his surprise, one of his co-workers received a deceptive program that spread from her computer to every computer in the office. Bobby's computer was infected and he could not finish his work. What sort of threat is Bobby experiencing?

   A) a virus

   B) spyware

   C) ransomware

3. Jennifer is used to seeing annoying pop-up ads appear when she is using Google Chrome as her Web browser. Usually, there is some type of product being advertised. Today, however, she receives a pop-up ad with a message that says that her computer is about to crash. No matter what she does, the pop-up ad will not go away. What sort of threat is Jennifer experiencing?

        A) a virus

        B) malware

        C) ransomware

4. Jill has noticed that every time she surfs the Internet, banner advertisements appear that reflect her Web surfing habits. She feels like she's being watched. What sort of threat is Jill experiencing?

        A) adware

        B) spyware

        C) ransomware

        D) a virus

        E) both A and B

5. Victor got a great deal on a popular antivirus software program released in 2015. The program received great reviews when it first became available for consumers to purchase. Victor installed the program on his computer. What mistake did Victor make in purchasing the software?

_____

_____

Key Terms

Android
A mobile operating system maintained by Google.

Antivirus Software
A program that shields the computer from harmful attacks by detecting and removing all threats and potential threats.

Chromebook
A small laptop designed to be used while connected to the Internet.

Chrome OS
An open-source operating system designed by Google that uses the Google Chrome Web browser as its user interface and mostly supports Web applications.

Firewall
A security system designed to block unauthorized access to or from a private network.

Font
A representation of text in a stylistic way.

Interface
The exchange of information among the hardware, software, humans, and the input and output devices connected to the computer.

iOS
The mobile operating system designed by Apple to run on its line of mobile devices.

Linux
A family of open-source operating systems that is freely available and can be modified by anyone around the world.

Malware
A program designed to harm a computer or device, short for malicious software.

Open-Source
A term that refers to software with source code that is available to the public to evaluate, modify, improve, and distribute.

Operating System
A program that manages the hardware and software on a computer.

Ransomware
Software that prevents access to a computer system until a sum of money is paid.

Spreadsheet
A computer application divided into rows and columns that manages data and performs different calculations.

Key Terms

Spyware
A program that can collect and transmit personal information about another's computer activities without the user being aware.

Template
A sample document that provides a useful layout for completing similar documents.

Tizen
An open-source operating system used primarily in smart appliances, wearable devices, in-car entertainment systems, televisions, and virtual reality headsets made by Samsung.

Virus
Computer code capable of damaging a system or destroying data.

Word Processing
The creation, editing, and formatting of text using computer software.

LESSON FOUR: Using the Internet

Introduction

Objectives – After completing this lesson, you will be able to:

- Browse the Internet
- Maximize your online searches
- Apply best practices for shopping on the Internet
- Pay bills using your bank's online bill paying services
- Deposit checks remotely using your mobile device
- Identify popular social media sites and their characteristics
- Practice good social media etiquette

Key Terms

- Bandwidth
- Broadband
- Home Page
- Internet
- Internet Service Provider
- Payee
- Remote Deposit Capture
- Search Engine
- Secure Sockets Layer
- Social Media
- Tweet
- Web Browser
- Wi-Fi Hotspot

What is the Internet?

The **Internet** is a global network of computers all connected to each other by telephone lines, cables, and satellites. Many refer to it as the "World Wide Web" or "the Net." People around the globe are able to exchange data, news, and opinions in seconds. It is possible to connect to the Internet through an **Internet Service Provider**, or ISP. Examples of ISPs include telecommunications companies and cable providers like AT&T, Verizon, and Comcast. If you have landline telephone service in your home, it is likely that your provider also offers access to the Internet. In fact, in many communities, **broadband,** or high-speed Internet access, has become a preferred service over traditional dial-up access to the Internet. The higher speeds offered by broadband are favored by consumers who want faster speeds for the latest devices, applications, and media that require larger bandwidths for data travel. **Bandwidth** is the rate of data transfer and is typically measured in bits per second. The table below presents common bandwidth abbreviations and their meaning.

Bandwidth Abbreviation	Meaning
Kbps	Kilobits per second. Generally used when referring to dialup Internet access.
Mbps	Megabits per second. The most common unit of speed used to describe bandwidth.
Gbps	Gigabits per second. The next generation of broadband Internet. Speeds reach 1,000 Mbps.

As you think about how you use the Internet, you can determine what type of broadband connection will best meet your needs. Having the right broadband connection can enhance productivity. Likewise, paying too much for speeds you do not need can unnecessarily add dollars to your Internet bill. If you do not use the Internet a lot and only perform basic, low-bandwidth tasks, a simple dial-up connection may be a reasonable, affordable option for accessing the Internet. The following information, which is based on rough estimates, will help you make a well-informed decision about the Internet connection speed you need.

Bandwidth Use	Reasonable Internet Connection Speed for Downloads
Surfing the internet	56 Kbps
Sending a text e-mail with no attachments	56 Kbps
Hanging out on Facebook	.5 Mbps
Sending an e-mail with attachments	1 Mbps
Watching a 10-minute YouTube video	1 Mbps
Downloading a high resolution image	1 Mbps
Playing a video game online for 30 minutes	1 Mbps
Streaming music	2 Mbps
Downloading a 2-hour movie	10 Mbps
Streaming a 4K video	15 to 25 Mbps

Source: Estimates based on data from OTT Communications

Once you have the right Internet connection along with the necessary hardware provided by your ISP, you can begin using the Internet. As we discussed in Lesson Two, a **Web browser** will give you access to the Internet and allow you to view Web pages on your computer. Popular Web browsers include Mozilla Firefox, Google Chrome, Microsoft Edge (formerly Internet Explorer), and Apple Safari (if using a MacIntosh computer). Each Web browser has its own toolbar. Toolbar buttons will help you move around Web sites and reload Web pages. Below is a quick reference guide for commonly used toolbar buttons.

Back   **Forward**   **Refresh**

- Click the **Back** button to go back to a page you have already visited.
- Click the **Forward** button to go to the page you were on before you pressed the back button.
- Click the **Refresh** button to reload or update a page you are on.

Everyday Tasks Made Easy

Searching the Web

The Internet makes it possible to search for just about anything. From apartments available for rent to new recipes and gardening tips, you can collect the information that is most relevant to you.

How do you search the Web?

1) First, open your Web browser.

2) Next, type the address of the search engine you want to use in the **address bar**, or select it from a bookmarks menu (i.e., saved shortcuts of your preferred locations on the Web – see Lesson Two), or list of favorites. A **search engine** is a tool that scans thousands of Web sites and Web pages to gather and organize the information you are seeking. Three of the most popular search engines are Google (www.google.com), Bing (www.bing.com), and Yahoo (www.yahoo.com). Some people make the search engine Web site their home page. The **home page** is the first page that appears whenever you open your browser.

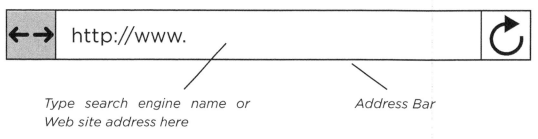

Type search engine name or Web site address here

Address Bar

3) Press the Enter key.

4) A search box, or search field, will show. Type key words into the search box and press the search button. The search button will look like a magnifying lens.

5) The results from your search will appear as a list of Web sites and links. The most relevant will be at the top of the list.

6) Carefully review the list.

7) To visit a site, click on the link that is most suitable for you.

Everyday Tasks Made Easy

Shopping

Shopping online is rapidly growing in popularity. Consumers are getting used to the benefits of convenience, choice, affordability, and faster delivery times for merchandise. According to Business Insider Intelligence, the online retail market in the United States is expected to reach $632 billion by 2020, which compares to $385 billion spent online in 2016. As more and more traditional retailers discover the advantages of selling products online, the options that consumers face are likely to skyrocket. With so many companies competing for dollars spent online, and cybercriminals waiting patiently to scam innocent victims, there are few things that you should know about shopping online.

Shopping Cart

1) **It's easy.** Many online retailers have their own search engines so that you can find what you need quickly. Simply add the items you want to your shopping cart and when you're done, proceed to checkout.

The checkout process will ask you for your billing and shipping address along with a valid credit card number, expiration date, and the three-digit security code on the back of the card. The retailer will apply the appropriate sales tax and shipping and handling fees. Once you submit the order, you will receive a confirmation number. If you choose to have your order delivered instead of picking up your merchandise at a nearby store, most online retailers will provide you with a tracking number to track your shipment.

2) **It can be safe.** Safety while shopping online ultimately depends on your choices. It should come as no surprise that some choices are better and safer than others. The following Dos and Don'ts will help you make the right online shopping decisions.

Online Shopping Tips

DO	DON'T
• **DO** shop at trusted Web sites that have a strong reputation. These sites are likely to have very good security measures in place.	• **DON'T** fall for offers that seem too good to be true, especially during the holidays.
• **DO** use a credit card instead of a debit card. Credit cards are not linked to your bank account and carry additional protections for consumers.	• **DON'T** provide your social security number or date of birth. This information is not needed and is usually desired by crooks.
• **DO** shop at a Web site that starts with **https://** instead of just **http://**. The "s" stands for **secure**.	• **DON'T** buy from a Web site that does not have SSL (**secure sockets layer**) encryption installed. SSL will keep your data private. Look for the SSL certificate symbol.
• **DO** shop at a Web site that has a padlock symbol at the beginning of the address bar. 	• **DON'T** make purchases while using public Wi-Fi. Many **Wi-Fi hotspots** are not secure.
• **DO** opt to use data provided by your service provider if you must shop online while you're out and about.	• **DON'T** give anyone your credit card number in an e-mail.

Activity #1

Directions: Read each question and provide the **best** answer.

1. Based on what you have learned about shopping online, which online retailer would be the best place to buy office supplies?

   A) Sam's Office Shack

   B) Office Depot

   C) Home Goods

2. What information appearing in the address bar indicates that the Web site is secure?

   A) http://

   B) ssl://

   C) https://

3. Which information is not needed during the checkout process?

   A) date of birth

   B) billing address

   C) credit card number

4. It's time to shop online! Number the following seven (7) steps in the correct order, with one (1) being the first step and seven (7) being the final step.

Step	Order (1 to 7)
Click the checkout button	
Track your package	
Submit your order	
Receive your merchandise	
Add items to your shopping cart	
Receive an order confirmation via e-mail	
Enter the shipping address and your credit card information	

Banking

Regardless of your age, as you manage your financial life, banking plays a very important part. Online banking offers convenience and flexibility that cannot be obtained by visiting a brick-and-mortar bank. There is automatic access to a record of your checking account transactions that helps you maintain a visual of your daily cash flows. Recurring bills can easily be paid online from your bank account, and you can move funds that reside at the same bank from one account to another. For example, you can transfer funds from a savings account or line of credit to a checking account. If you have a credit card with your bank, you can pay off a balance by simply transferring funds from your checking account to your credit card account.

Accessing your bank account online requires that you register with your bank to conduct online banking. Typically, you can register at your bank's Web site or download your bank's app to your mobile device. In each instance, you must provide a username, password, and answers to security, or challenge, questions. Your username should be something that you can easily remember and the password should be a series of characters (including letters, numbers, and symbols) that would be difficult for someone to figure out. We will discuss what constitutes a strong password in more detail in Lesson Six.

Security questions are designed to protect your account. Here are a few tips for choosing your security questions and answers.

- Choose questions with answers that you can remember in the future and answer consistently.
- Use one-word answers whenever possible.
- Be careful with spaces. If you use "Las Vegas" as an answer to one of your security questions, most systems will reject "LasVegas" and "Vegas."
- Pick a question which cannot be easily guessed or researched and has many possible answers.
- Select a question for which the answer is unlikely to be known by others such as a family member, close friend, relative, ex-spouse, or significant other.
- Choose a question having an answer not likely to change over time.
- **Remember S-M-S-M-S.**
  - **Simple** – has a one-word answer
  - **Memorable** – easy to remember
  - **Stable** – does not change over time
  - **Multiple** – many answers are possible
  - **Safe** – unlikely to be known by others and cannot be figured out easily

If you need assistance with the online registration process, call or visit your bank. A bank representative will be more than happy to help you get started online because the more routine services you complete online, the less staff and paper resources you will need, which will ultimately save the bank time and money.

Activity #2

Directions: Below are sample security questions, many of which are used for password resets. Answer each question, noting whether **simple**, **memorable**, **stable**, **multiple**, and **safe** (S-M-S-M-S) applies to the question and your answer. Circle the S-M-S-M-S characteristics that apply.

1. Which phone number do you remember most from your childhood?

   Answer: _____

       Simple   Memorable   Stable   Multiple   Safe

2. What is the nickname of your childhood best friend?

   Answer: _____

       Simple   Memorable   Stable   Multiple   Safe

3. What was your high school mascot?

   Answer: _____

       Simple   Memorable   Stable   Multiple   Safe

4. What is your mother's maiden name?

   Answer: _____

       Simple   Memorable   Stable   Multiple   Safe

5. What was the make of your first car?

   Answer: _____

       Simple   Memorable   Stable   Multiple   Safe

6. In what city were you born?

   Answer: _____

       Simple   Memorable   Stable   Multiple   Safe

7. In what town did you meet your spouse or significant other?

Answer: _____

    Simple   Memorable   Stable   Multiple   Safe

8. What is your favorite color?

Answer: _____

    Simple   Memorable   Stable   Multiple   Safe

9. What is your father's middle name?

Answer: _____

    Simple   Memorable   Stable   Multiple   Safe

10. What is the last name of the teacher who gave you your first failing grade?

Answer: _____

    Simple   Memorable   Stable   Multiple   Safe

11. What is your grandmother's first name?

Answer: _____

    Simple   Memorable   Stable   Multiple   Safe

12. What is the name of the elementary or grammar school you attended?

Answer: _____

    Simple   Memorable   Stable   Multiple   Safe

Which questions/answers had the most number of S-M-S-M-S characteristics circled? These questions are likely to be the best and safest ones to use as challenge questions, as it is likely to be more difficult for someone to access your bank account by guessing or researching your answers.

The R.E.E.L.

The ability to pay bills online is a great option for banking customers. Whether you're settling a bill with your electricity provider, cable provider, credit card company, or doctor, you can pay balances owed with automatic payments or payments sent on a schedule that you choose.

The brief exercise below will jumpstart the process of paying bills online.

Directions: Obtain a copy of a current bill and answer each of the following questions. Refer to your answers when you set up payment information online.

Bill Information

1) Who is the payee? _____

2) What is the address of the payee? _____

3) What is your account number? _____

4) What amount do you want to pay? _____

5) When do you want the money to be taken out of your checking account? (provide a date or frequency schedule) _____

Note: The **payee** is the company or individual to whom money is to be paid.

Howie's How-Tos on Depositing Checks Remotely

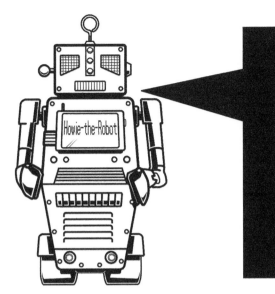

Follow these twelve (12) simple steps for depositing checks with a mobile device, also known as *remote deposit capture*. Keep in mind that exact steps will vary slightly based on your bank's mobile app and features.

1) Download your bank's mobile app.

2) Log on, entering your username and password.

3) Use the menu to select the "Deposit Checks" option (sign up for the service if you have not already done so).

4) Choose an account to deposit your check.

5) Take a picture of the front of the check, making sure that all four corners are included in the picture. (Most apps will have a photo button for the "Front ofCheck" and "Back of Check")

6) Take a picture of the back of the check, making sure that you have properly endorsed the back of the check with your signature and "For Deposit Only."

7) Review the check images on your phone for clarity.

8) Verify the amount of the check deposit.

9) Select the Submit button.

10) Choose to deposit another check or simply review the deposit receipt.

11) Await an e-mail from your bank confirming the transaction.

12) Securely store your check for five days in case problems occur.

Using Social Media

Interesting Statistics:

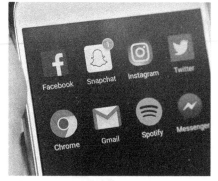

- 7 in 10 Americans use social media to connect
  (Source: Pew Research Center, January 2017)
- Facebook has over 2 billion active users monthly
  (Source: Facebook.com Newsroom, June 2017)
- 59% of 18-29 year olds use Instagram
  (Source: Pew Research Center, January 2017)
- 49% of college graduates use LinkedIn
  (Source: Pew Research Center, January 2017)
- 70% of employers use social media to screen job candidates
  (Source: CareerBuilder, June 2017)

Social media has become a way of communicating and bringing together communities that were once geographically cut off. Users from around the world create and share content and interact with one another.

What exactly is social media?

Social media consists of Web sites and applications that encourage the sharing of information and opinions. Social media facilitates connections with family, friends, classmates, employers, and customers. These connections are called social networks.

What are some examples of social media sites and their unique characteristics?

Site	What happens?
Facebook	Users create profiles, upload photos and video, send messages, and keep in touch with family, friends, and colleagues.
Twitter	Users post short messages to the world daily using a hash, or pound, sign (#) that precedes the message. Each post is called a **tweet**.
Instagram	Users share photos and videos from a smartphone.
LinkedIn	Users share professional information. Considered a business social network.
Pinterest	Users upload, save, sort, and manage pins (also known as images) through collections called pinboards.
YouTube	Users upload videos to be viewed by users and nonusers alike.

Now that you know what social media is and how you can use different social media platforms for your benefit, you can engage with others in an informed way. It is hard to know who may be watching or following your behavior, so be wise and be safe. Here are a few Social Media Dos and Don'ts to help keep you on the straight and narrow path.

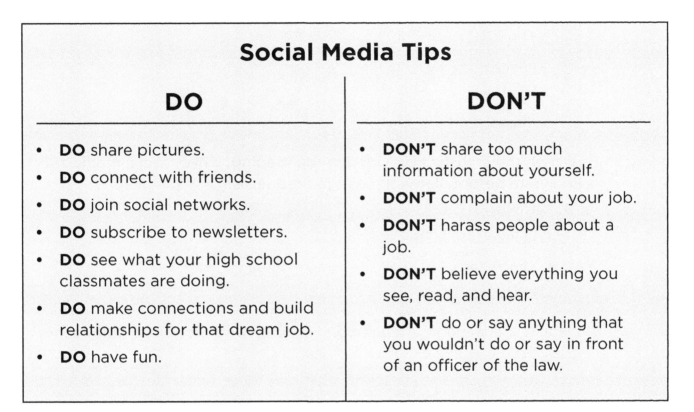

Social Media Tips

DO

- **DO** share pictures.
- **DO** connect with friends.
- **DO** join social networks.
- **DO** subscribe to newsletters.
- **DO** see what your high school classmates are doing.
- **DO** make connections and build relationships for that dream job.
- **DO** have fun.

DON'T

- **DON'T** share too much information about yourself.
- **DON'T** complain about your job.
- **DON'T** harass people about a job.
- **DON'T** believe everything you see, read, and hear.
- **DON'T** do or say anything that you wouldn't do or say in front of an officer of the law.

Activity #3

Directions: Read each question and provide the **best** answer.

1. Based on the statistics provided in the reading, which social media site is known to be highly popular with young adults (i.e., 18-29 year olds)?

   A) LinkedIn

   B) Facebook

   C) Twitter

   D) Instagram

2. Based on the statistics provided in the reading, which social media site is known to be popular with college graduates?

   A) Twitter

   B) LinkedIn

   C) Facebook

   D) Pinterest

3. On which social media site are you likely to tweet about current events?

   A) YouTube

   B) Pinterest

   C) Twitter

   D) Instagram

4. Which social media networking site is the most widely-used among all age groups?

   A) Pinterest

   B) LinkedIn

   C) YouTube

   D) Facebook

5. Which social media site is often referred to as a business social network?

        A) LinkedIn

        B) Pinterest

        C) Twitter

        D) Instagram

6. When using social media, why is it important to keep your digital life separate from your personal life?

_____

_____

_____

_____

7. When using social media, why is it important <u>not</u> to trust too easily?

_____

_____

_____

_____

Key Terms

Bandwidth — The rate of data transfer measured in bits per second.

Broadband — High-speed Internet access.

Home Page — A Web page set as the initial page that comes into view after opening the browser.

Internet — A global network of computers all connected to each other by telephone lines, cables, and satellites.

Internet Service Provider (ISP) — A company that provides access to the Internet.

Payee — The company or individual to whom money is to be paid.

Remote Deposit Capture (RDC) — A service that allows a customer to scan checks remotely and transmit the check images safely to a bank for deposit.

Search Engine — A tool that scans thousands of Web sites and Web pages to gather and organize the information that is most relevant.

Secure Sockets Layer (SSL) — Security technology that ensures that all data passing between the Web server and browsers is kept private.

Social Media — Web sites and applications that encourage the sharing of information and opinions.

Tweet — A posting made on Twitter. Also, to make a posting on Twitter.

Web Browser — A software application that provides access to the Internet and allows you to view Web pages on your computer.

Wi-Fi Hotspot — A place that allows computers, smartphones, and other devices to connect to the Internet wirelessly; examples include cafes, libraries, hotels, and airports.

Introduction

Objectives – After completing this lesson, you will be able to:

- Use e-mail features effectively
- Send and receive e-mail
- Send attachments
- Recognize common e-mail folders

Key Terms

- Blind Carbon Copy (Bcc)
- Carbon Copy (Cc)
- Domain
- E-mail
- Forward
- Inbox
- Reply
- Spam E-mail

What is E-mail?

E-mail, or electronic mail, is a quick way of sending messages to others using the Internet. E-mail can be sent to one individual or a group of individuals. Similar to sending a letter, an address is required in order to receive an e-mail. However, unlike the regular postal system, both the sender and the recipient must have an e-mail address that no one else has. This unique e-mail address serves as an electronic post office box that identifies the e-mail user. The e-mail address consists of three main parts: a username, the "@", or "at", symbol, and a **domain**. The username can represent a person's name, a nickname, a personal interest, or some other special identifier. A username can also represent a combination of letters and numbers. For example, the username johndoe7 might represent a first and last name (e.g., John Doe) along with a favorite number of seven or a reference to being born on the seventh day of the month. Many people have a professional e-mail address for their place of work and a separate e-mail address for personal use, so don't feel like you're limited to only one e-mail address.

The domain comes after the @ symbol and represents the network that is linked to the Internet. Examples of a domain include company.com, company.org, school.edu, and state.gov. Combining the username with the @ symbol and domain provides the complete e-mail address. In our example, the e-mail address might be johndoe7@company.com.

Activity #1

Directions: It's time to check your understanding of an e-mail address. Read each question. Circle the **best** answer.

1. Which of the following symbols represents the "at" symbol?

    A) #

    B) &

    C) @

2. Which of the following is not a main part of an e-mail address?

    A) the password

    B) the username

    C) the domain

3. Which of the following is an example of a valid e-mail address?

    A) johnsmith@nyc.gov

    B) scorpio22@gmail.com

    C) pjones@californiacolleges.edu

    D) All of the above

4. **True** or **False**. Write **T** for True or **F** for False next to the statements below.

    _____ a) It is possible to have the same e-mail address as a relative who shares your last name.

    _____ b) You can have more than one e-mail address.

    _____ c) It is not possible to have an e-mail address that ends in ".org".

Sending and Receiving E-mail

Figure 5-1: Dan's Electronic Mailbox

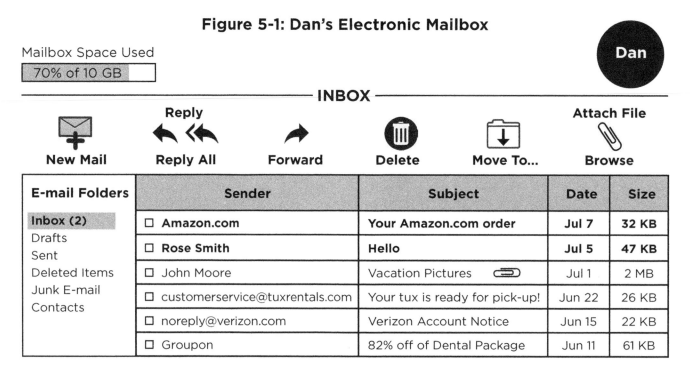

Most e-mail services will provide you with an electronic mailbox. The electronic mailbox includes a number of features that will help organize the e-mails that you send and receive while also allowing you to perform specific tasks. These features will differ slightly depending on the e-mail provider, but there are some tools that are generally the same regardless of the service provider. The **inbox** folder will house the e-mails that you receive and the **sent** folder will keep a copy of the e-mails that you send. In most instances, e-mails that you have not opened will appear in bold. In **Figure 5-1**, there are two unopened e-mails in Dan's inbox. One is from Amazon.com and the other is from Rose Smith. When Dan goes into his inbox, he can see who sent him a message under the **sender** field and what the message is about under the **subject** field. He can also view the date the message was sent along with the size of the message. If a particular e-mail has an attachment, there will usually be a paperclip symbol. In **Figure 5-1**, Dan has received an attachment from John Moore. Given the subject of the message, this attachment is most likely pictures from a recent vacation.

Dan can open his e-mail by clicking once on the subject line. Some e-mail programs will also allow you to open an e-mail by clicking on the sender's name. Once the e-mail is open, Dan can choose to respond to the sender by clicking on the "Reply" button or he can forward the e-mail to another person by clicking on the "Forward" button. Some e-mail programs will have an arrow pointing toward the left for replying and an arrow pointing towards the right for forwarding. Dan can also delete the message or simply choose not to respond. It is important to keep in mind that some "Delete" buttons will look like a trash can and may not have a label attached letting you know that it is a "delete" function. If you see a trash can icon, be assured that you can click on the icon to delete a message that you would like to remove from a particular folder in your electronic mailbox.

Figure 5-2: Dan's Reply

Send	New Mail	Reply / Reply All	Forward	Delete	Move To...	Attach File / Browse

E-mail Folders	To:	John Moore
Inbox	Cc:	Sue
Drafts	**Subject:**	Re: Vacation Pictures
Sent	**Message:**	Hi John,
Deleted Items		Thanks for sending the vacation pictures. I can see that you and your family had lots of fun. I will share these with Sue. Say hello to Kim and the boys.
Junk E-mail		Take care,
Contacts		Dan

If Dan chooses to respond to John Moore, for example, a new e-mail will open and the "To," or address, field will already be completed. The subject field will also be completed and start with "**Re**." "Re" stands for reply or response. Dan can type his message in the main body of the e-mail. He can also send a copy to Sue by clicking on the "To" or "Cc" button and selecting the e-mail address for Sue. If Dan clicks on the "To" button, Sue's e-mail address will be added alongside John Moore's e-mail address. If he clicks on the "Cc" button, Sue's e-mail address will be placed in the Cc field. Cc stands for **carbon copy** and allows you to send a copy of the e-mail message to all the individuals added to the Cc field. Alternatively, some e-mail applications will automatically provide the e-mail address of a recipient in your list of contacts if you begin typing the individual's name or part of his or her e-mail address. Usually, e-mail addresses with similar names or characters will appear. Then you will have an opportunity to select the e-mail address of the person you would like to send an e-mail.

Most e-mail programs also provide a **blind carbon copy** option. The blind carbon copy, or Bcc, option allows you to send copies of the e-mail message to other individuals without the recipients in the To or Cc field being aware. The blind carbon copy feature also makes it possible to send multiple individuals the same message without broadcasting the e-mail addresses of everyone on the recipient list. This is a beneficial option when you want to keep the e-mail addresses of your contacts private, or you want to prevent others from knowing who you have included in an e-mail. Finally, Dan can send his e-mail by clicking the "Send" button.

If Dan wants to share the pictures that John Moore sent with Sue, he can forward John's original e-mail to Sue by clicking on the "Forward" button. Again, a new e-mail will open, but the subject field will show "FW" to indicate that the message is being forwarded. In this case, the "To" field will be blank, so Dan will have to click on the "To" button and select Sue's e-mail address from his list of contacts or begin typing Sue's name so that a list of possible e-mail addresses will appear for his choosing.

Figure 5-3: Dan's New Message

E-mail Folders	To:	robin.ward@yahoo.com
Inbox	Cc:	
Drafts	Subject:	Coffee Tomorrow?
Sent	Message:	Hi Robin,
Deleted Items		Are you available for coffee tomorrow at 8:30 a.m.? I was hoping we could meet at Joe's Coffee Shop on Main Street. Let me know. I look forward to seeing you!
Junk E-mail		
Contacts		Dan

If Dan simply wants to create a new e-mail instead of responding to or forwarding an e-mail in his inbox, he can do so by clicking on "New Mail." Some e-mail programs will use the word "Compose" or "Write" as a command button for creating a new e-mail message, so be on the lookout for these alternative ways of crafting your message. When a new e-mail opens, the "To" field and the subject field will be blank. You will have to type or select the recipient's name or e-mail address for the "To" field. In **Figure 5-3**, Dan has chosen to send an e-mail to Robin Ward and has typed in her entire e-mail address in the "To" field.

It is important to keep in mind that you will not be able to send an e-mail without a valid recipient's e-mail address. If the e-mail address is not valid, you will receive an error message from your e-mail service provider. While typing in a valid e-mail address is required, typing information in the subject field is optional. However, many people receiving e-mail use the information in the subject field to determine the content, safety, and urgency of an e-mail message. If you want a faster response from the person you are sending an e-mail message, it is helpful to type a word or two that indicates what your e-mail is about. In **Figure 5-3**, Dan lets Robin know that his message is about having coffee tomorrow.

After completing the "To" and subject fields, you can type your message and press the "Send" button to send the e-mail.

Activity #2

Directions: Maria has chosen to open a free e-mail account using Google Mail, or Gmail. Initially, however, Maria makes a few mistakes. Read each scenario and provide a response that would help Maria with the correct use of e-mail.

Scenario 1:

Maria chooses a username for herself that's exactly the same as her cousin Stella's.

What should Maria have done differently?

_____

_____

Scenario 2:

Maria is completely set up and has a valid e-mail address. She sends a test e-mail to her best friend Patty. After sending the e-mail to Patty, she looks for a copy of that e-mail in her inbox.

What should Maria have done differently?

_____

_____

Scenario 3:

Maria has received a response back from Patty. She immediately responds to Patty's e-mail by clicking on the "Forward" button.

What should Maria have done differently?

_____

_____

Scenario 4:

Maria wants to draft a new e-mail to her Uncle Chuck about an upcoming family reunion. She clicks on the "Send" button to draft the e-mail.

What should Maria have done differently?

_____

_____

Scenario 5:

Maria begins drafting her e-mail message to her Uncle Chuck. She types "Family Reunion" in the subject field and types her letter in the message field. She clicks "Send," but an error message appears saying that the e-mail cannot be sent.

What should Maria have done differently?

_____

_____

Sending Attachments

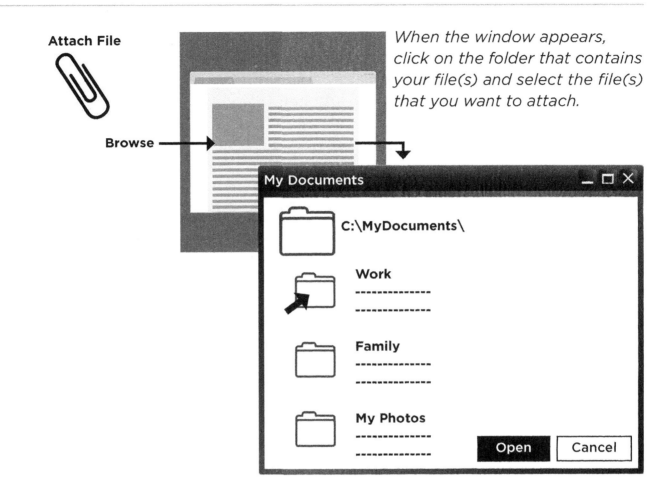

Attach File

Browse

When the window appears, click on the folder that contains your file(s) and select the file(s) that you want to attach.

My Documents

C:\MyDocuments\

Work

Family

My Photos

Open   Cancel

As mentioned earlier in this lesson, the **paperclip** symbol indicates an e-mail attachment. An attachment is simply a type of file such as a photograph, document, or spreadsheet. Attaching files to an e-mail provides a quick way of sending information that is stored on your computer. When you click on the "Attach File" button, a new window will appear that shows the folders and files on your computer. Find the file you want to include in the e-mail and select it. Depending on the e-mail program, you may have to click "OK" or "Open" for the file to appear in your e-mail message. If you have followed these steps correctly, the name of the file that you selected will show as an attachment in your e-mail message. Also, you are not limited to sending only one file. You can select multiple files to send in one e-mail. Simply click on the "Attach File" button and follow the same process for each file that you want to send. Sending files that are very large in size will impact the transmission speed of those files. In other words, the larger the file size, the slower the transmission speed. Photographs, for example, will take a little longer to send than a resume or favorite recipe in a Word document.

Directions: Assume that you have typed a valid e-mail address in the "To" field for someone you would like to send an e-mail attachment. Correctly order the following steps for attaching an e-mail attachment from one (1) to five (5) with one being the first step and five being the last step.

Step	Order (1 to 5)
Click "Send"	
Select the file you want to include in the e-mail	
Click "OK" or "Open"	
Find the file you want to include in the e-mail	
Click on the "Attach File" button or paperclip symbol	

E-mail Folders

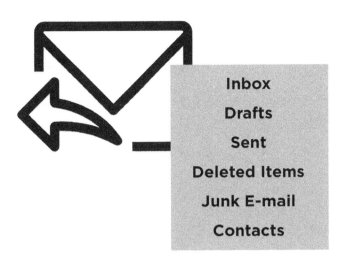

In addition to the **inbox** and **sent** folders discussed earlier in this lesson, there are a few other e-mail folders that you may find useful. The "Drafts" folder will save a copy of e-mail messages that you start, but never finish or send. The "Deleted Items" folder will keep a copy of e-mails that you no longer need and have deleted. E-mail items in this folder can be permanently removed from your electronic mailbox by deleting each item in this folder.

The "Junk E-mail" folder contains spam e-mail. **Spam e-mail** is e-mail that is sent to a large group of people in a way that is difficult to determine who the sender is. Many times the sender of spam e-mail is an advertiser, but sometimes the sender is someone who is trying to access information on your computer without your permission. Many e-mail programs are able to detect whether an e-mail is spam or not and will automatically place suspicious e-mail in the "Junk" folder. However, it is possible for legitimate e-mails to slip through. Thus, it is important to check the "Junk E-mail" folder on a regular basis to determine whether valid e-mails may have gone into your junk folder. It is also a good practice to delete any e-mails in your junk folder where you do not recognize the e-mail address of the sender.

Finally, the "Contacts" folder stores the e-mail addresses and contact information of your family, friends, and colleagues.

Activity #4

Directions: Read each statement about using e-mail folders and decide whether you agree or disagree with it. Circle your answer.

1. The "Junk E-mail" folder can contain both spam e-mails and legitimate e-mails.

   Agree   Disagree

2. The "Drafts" folder stores the e-mail addresses and contact information of family, friends, and colleagues.

   Agree   Disagree

3. You should be very cautious of spam e-mails and e-mails from people you don't know.

   Agree   Disagree

4. When you delete an e-mail in your inbox, it is permanently removed from your electronic mailbox.

   Agree   Disagree

5. If you start an e-mail and want to finish it later, you can save it and come back to it at another time.

   Agree   Disagree

Key Terms

Blind Carbon Copy (Bcc)
A way of sending an e-mail to individuals without the recipients being aware of who is on the distribution list or knowing the e-mail addresses of the other recipients.

Carbon Copy (Cc)
A way of sending a copy of an e-mail message to individuals other than those selected to the "To" field. All recipients are aware of who is receiving the e-mail message.

Domain
The part of the e-mail address that represents the network that is linked to the Internet.

E-mail
Quick way of sending messages to others using the Internet, also referred to as electronic mail.

Forward
Sending an e-mail that has been received to another recipient.

Inbox
The folder in an e-mail program that houses incoming e-mails.

Reply
Sending an e-mail response back to the person that sent the e-mail.

Spam E-mail
E-mail that is sent to a large group of people in a way that is difficult to determine who the sender is. Many times the sender of spam e-mail is an advertiser, but sometimes the sender is someone who is trying to access information on a person's computer without their permission.

LESSON SIX: Online Safety & Privacy

Introduction

Objectives – After completing this lesson, you will be able to:

- Recognize signs that your computer has been hacked
- Recover from a hack
- Recover from identity theft
- Guard against hackers
- Create a strong password
- Identify suspicious e-mails
- Understand how cookies are used to track your Internet activity
- Protect your online privacy

Key Terms

- Cookie
- Cybercriminal
- Cyber Threat Actor (CTA)
- Data Breach
- Ethernet Cable
- Hack
- Hacker
- Malware
- Phishing Scam
- Product Key
- Unsecured Wireless Network

Hackers and Malware

When most people hear the word "hacker," negative thoughts come to mind. Typically, hackers are associated with computer viruses, massive network outings, online criminal activity, and identity theft. It is hard to imagine a hacker being connected with anything good. However, hackers are actually known for their sharp computer skills and know-how. They are often called upon to fix technical problems and find flaws in large computer systems. Despite the good that some hackers do, there is reason to be alarmed when hearing the word "hacker." Most hackers' intentions are not meant to be helpful, but meant to cause harm. In fact, a computer **hacker** is someone who tries to get unauthorized access to your computer in order to obtain information that can be used for personal gain. Some hackers are so cunning that victims are not aware that their computer system is being illegally accessed, or **hacked**. What are some signs that your computer is being hacked?

1) You can't download the latest antivirus program.
2) Your computer runs unusually slow.
3) A well-known company was recently hacked.
4) Your computer hard drive seems to be working overtime, making a low, continuous sound that is different than normal.
5) Your antivirus software turns off by itself.
6) Strange things are happening on your screen.
7) Your computer is doing things by itself.

If you cannot update your computer with the latest antivirus program, malware may be the reason. As discussed in Lesson Three, **malware** is a type of malicious software that harms your computer. Hackers use malware to prevent system updates, disable your antivirus program, and search for data on your computer to damage or steal. Malware can get into your computer without you being aware. For example, clicking on a misleading ad, going to an unsafe Web site, or downloading an infected document can cause malware to enter your computer system.

If you notice that your Internet connection has slowed, it is possible that a hacker is using your bandwidth, particularly if you have an **unsecured wireless network** in your home. An unsecured wireless network provides access to the Internet without having to enter a password.

As an additional alert, it is important to pay attention to current events involving well-known companies that have been hacked. If hackers were able to get e-mail addresses and passwords from these companies, they will test this information on a variety of computer systems in an attempt to obtain unauthorized access. Also, many times hackers gain access to personal information such as social security numbers and addresses in an attempt to make illegal purchases or sell this information to other criminals.

Finally, be on the look out for strange things appearing on your computer screen. If you see new icons or programs on your desktop that you have not seen before, it is likely that you've been hacked. Also, if your computer seems to have a mind of its own and your cursor moves without you controlling it, you have every right to be alarmed. Someone else is likely operating your computer from another location, which could be anywhere in the world.

If you suspect that your computer has been hacked, do not panic. Instead, take action to keep your files from being damaged and prevent your computer from being used to attack other computers. Immediately, put on the mindset of a level-headed individual who will not suffer defeat or let the **cybercriminal** triumph. Use the following seven (7) steps to recover from a hack and get back on offense!

1) **Pull the network cable on your computer and turn off the Internet connection.** This action will cut ties with the hacker. The network cable, also called **Ethernet cable**, connects your computer to your high speed Internet.

Network Cable

2) **Shut down your computer.** In other words, turn it off.

3) **Take your computer to a trusted computer repair shop** and have the computer technician scan your computer for malware. He or she should also back up your personal files.

4) Once all your personal files are backed up, **wipe the hard drive clean** with a program that will erase everything that is on your hard drive.

5) **Reload the operating system.** Use the original disks that you purchased and download all updates. If no disks came with your computer, go to the manufacturer's Web site (e.g., Microsoft if using Windows), and download the operating system from the secure Web site. Remember, look for **https://**. You may need your product key, defined in Step 6, to verify your purchase.

6) **Reinstall your software,** including antivirus programs. If you do not have the physical disks, download the software using the product key that you were given when you initially purchased the software. The **product key** is a specialized code for licensed software that certifies that the copy of the program is original. Typically, the product key can be found on the label, so always keep a copy of the packaging materials that contain the label.

PRODUCT KEY: XXXXX-XXXXX-XXXXX-XXXXX-XXXXX

---

7) **Scan your backup files for viruses** before copying them back to your computer. Rescanning your files is an extra security measure to ensure that you do not put infected files on your newly cleaned hard drive.

Now that you are aware of the signs that your computer has been hacked and know how to recover successfully from a hack, here are a few tips to protect your computer from future hacks.

Tips to Avoid Being Hacked

DO	DON'T
• **DO** keep your computer's firewall turned on.	• **DON'T** open e-mail attachments unless you are super, super certain of where they came from.
• **DO** secure your wireless Internet connection with a strong password (discussed later).	• **DON'T** visit mysterious Web sites.
• **DO** conduct business with companies willing to protect your personal information and privacy.	• **DON'T** click on unfamiliar links.
• **DO** monitor your computer for unusual activity and noise.	• **DON'T** share personal information on public Wi-Fi networks (e.g., hotels, coffee shops, libraries, and conference centers).
• **DO** visit Web sites that are secure. Remember to look for **https://** and the padlock symbol.	• **DON'T** forget to **log out** of your accounts when you're done using them and **log off** a computer when you're finished using it.

Howie's How-Tos on Overcoming a Data Breach

Unfortunately, cyber attacks and data breaches are becoming facts of life. Even if a company has the best security tools and practices, hackers can still take advantage of human weaknesses. To make matters worse, there is a price tag attached to sensitive information. Medical records, credit card details, driver's license numbers, and personal passwords can earn hackers a nice amount of loot. In fact, some hackers are raking it in. If you or a company that you do business with have been hacked, the following actions will help you protect your identity and personal information.

1) Review your credit reports and account statements for unauthorized activity. Are there new accounts in your name or illegal purchases?

2) Request a free copy of your credit report by calling call 1-877-322-8228 or go online at www.annualcreditreport.com. You are entitled to one free copy each year from Equifax, Experian, and Transunion — the three main credit reporting agencies.

3) Report any unauthorized activity to your bank and/or credit card company.

4) If you see new charges on your accounts, place a freeze on the account or close the account to prevent additional charges.

5) Change logins, passwords, and PINs (Personal Identification Numbers) as necessary.

6) Report identity theft to the Federal Trade Commission (FTC) at www.IdentityTheft.gov or call 1-877-438-4338. The agency will create an Identity Theft Report and recovery plan for you.

7) Contact your local police department and file a report.

8) Take corrective measures: close new accounts opened in your name, remove unauthorized charges from your accounts, and correct your credit reports with each credit reporting agency.

Activity #1

Directions: Read each question. Circle the **best** answer.

1. Which of the following is not a sign that your computer is being hacked?

    A) Your computer is doing things by itself.

    B) Your antivirus software turns off by itself.

    C) It takes a few minutes to download the latest antivirus program.

    D) Your computer runs unusually slow.

2. Hackers can make a great sum of money selling which of the following items about you?

    A) your address

    B) your home telephone number

    C) your e-mail address

    D) your medical records

3. If you are a victim of identity theft, which of the following entities will create an Identity Theft Report and recovery plan for you?

    A) Equifax

    B) Federal Trade Commission

    C) Transunion

    D) Experian

4. Which of the following is a corrective course of action to protect your identity?

    A) close new accounts opened in your name

    B) request a free copy of your credit report

    C) delete all the files on your computer

    D) only visit mysterious Web sites when you are on a computer at your local library

5. **True** or **False**. Write **T** for True or **F** for False next to the statements below.

_____
a) You should open an e-mail attachment if you are 75% certain of where it came from.

_____
b) It is okay to share personal information on your hotel's Wi-Fi network.

_____
c) You will always know when malware has invaded your computer system.

6. Tyler can't download the latest antivirus program and his computer all of sudden freezes. He suspects that his computer has been hacked and needs to protect it from any further damage. What should he do? Plan a course of action for Tyler using the steps below. Correctly order each step from one (1) to seven (7) with one being the first step and seven being the last step.

Step	Order (1 to 7)
Shut down the computer	
Reinstall all software	
Take the computer to a trusted repair shop	
Scan all backup files for viruses	
Wipe the hard drive clean	
Pull the network cable on the computer	
Reload the operating system	

Strong Passwords

Nowadays, just about every online account requires a username and password. From e-mail to employment sites to social media, the list of entities requesting users to login to access specific information keeps growing. With data breaches being common and hackers with ill will lurking around every corner, being safe online requires having a strong password. Here are a few password requirements to keep your Internet accounts secure.

Your password must:

- ✓ Have at least one letter
- ✓ Have at least one capital letter
- ✓ Have at least one number
- ✓ Have at least one symbol, if allowed (some account services do not allow symbols)
- ✓ Not contain multiple identical consecutive characters (e.g., vBay2w777)
- ✓ Not be the same as your username
- ✓ Be at least nine (9) characters
- ✓ Not be a common password like "12345678" or "football"
- ✓ Not be an obvious dictionary word like "purple" or a combination of words like "purplelady"
- ✓ Not be used in the past year

Additionally, it is important to avoid storing a list of passwords in a saved file on your computer. Hackers can access this file and obtain all of your passwords. Also, do not use the same password for multiple accounts. Change the characters in your password in a way that you can easily remember. Lastly, be sure to change passwords frequently, particularly for e-mail and online banking accounts.

Activity #2

1. The list below contains twelve (12) potential passwords. Circle the **strong** passwords using the information you have learned about creating a secure password.

    987654321=   Password1   #71Dwq83Pfn   starwars

    bw?39P7dxp   flower   baseball   Trustno1

    dragon   mZ26=f391B   princess   s94U$G593h

2. Creating a strong password that you can easily remember can be difficult. Some people think of a phrase or sentence and change that phrase or sentence into letters, numbers, and symbols in order to form a strong password. For example, "**Emily, for you I'd go to jail**" can be transformed into **MLE,4uIdgo2jl**. Read each sentence below aloud, paying close attention to the sounds made. Make a strong password using the sounds that you hear. Use letters (both capital and lower case), numbers, and symbols, where applicable.

    a) I'd hate to go for you

    _____

    b) You are wonderful too!

    _____

    c) Do you know anyone?

    _____

    d) I see a canine cutie for me!

    _____

Suspicious E-mails

Figure 6-1: Dana's Suspicious E-mail

Send	New Mail	Reply / Reply All	Forward	Delete	Move To...	Attach File / Browse

E-mail Folders	From:	New Bank Security
Inbox		
Drafts	**Subject:**	Your account security is at risk
Sent	**Message:**	Dear Sir/Madam,
Deleted Items		Your information for your account has been compromised.
Junk E-mail		Please take immediate action to secure your personal information. Visit this **link** to update your login and password so that you can receive new credit card information.
Contacts		Kind regards,
		New Bank Security Team

Are you able to recognize suspicious e-mails? Cybercriminals often use fake e-mails with harmful links and attachments to break into personal accounts and attack computer systems. These fake e-mails are also referred to as a phishing (pronounced "fishing") scam. A phishing scam is an attempt through electronic means to get confidential or sensitive information from someone in a dishonest way. Typically, phishing is carried out through a fake e-mail or text message similar to the one shown in **Figure 6-1**. The message appears to be from a familiar company like a bank or service provider. The bank name and logo will be present, but there will also be instructions to click on a link and update your account details or personal information. Alternatively, there could be an attachment with a computer virus. There may be instructions in the message to open the attachment in order to receive a job offer, complete a survey, win a prize, receive a gift certificate, or participate in some other well-crafted scheme.

If you receive what you believe to be a phishing e-mail, do not click on any links or open any attachments. Check the incoming e-mail address to make sure it matches the Web site you think it is from. In most instances, the fake e-mail will have a different domain and will not be from the Web site that you suspect. For example, instead of being from your bank and having a .com domain, it might have a .org domain name or an unrecognizable country code (e.g., .uk for United Kingdom or .tw for Taiwan). The phishing e-mail could also show a friend's name or the name of someone in your address book. However, a closer look at the e-mail address will show a different domain name. Therefore, carefully examine all e-mail messages. Never open a file attachment unless you are absolutely certain that the sender is who he or she says. Also, never confirm your account number, PIN, password, or any other sensitive information via e-mail. As a security measure, banks and other service providers will never ask you to confirm this information in an e-mail.

During times of natural disasters and other high profile events, it is also possible to receive suspicious e-mails from cyber threat actors. **Cyber threat actors** can include hackers, cybercriminals, and phony organizations. These entities want you to think that they are acting on behalf of the well-being of others. They often request donations for disaster relief, particularly when there is a severe hurricane, tornado, or earthquake that causes massive devastation to a certain area. They also like to exploit human emotions and will try and lure you with pictures, videos, and pleas for immediate action. In such circumstances, it is important to verify whether the disaster relief effort is legitimate before clicking on any Web site links or attachments or providing any financial assistance. It is best not to act on emotion. Instead, visit the National Voluntary Organizations Active in Disaster Web site at **https://www.nvoad.org** to review a list of disaster relief organizations that have been thoroughly checked. Also, do your own research to confirm that the funds received by these organizations are being used to help those most in need of assistance.

Activity #3

Directions: Carefully review the suspicious e-mail referenced in **Figure 6-2** and answer the questions that follow.

Figure 6-2: Andrew's Suspicious E-mail

Send	New Mail	Reply / Reply All	Forward	Delete	Move To...	Attach File / Browse

E-mail Folders		
Inbox Drafts Sent Deleted Items Junk E-mail Contacts	**From:**	New Bank Online (alerts@notify.newbank.tw)
	Subject:	You Have 1 New Update
	Message:	You have 1 ONLINE account update, Use the proceed link to update your Profile to enable us add secure Authentication. (Reference Id: WF_SEPT-04_AUGB062100). Proceed to Update **Here**

1. What information in the sender's e-mail address is a red flag that the e-mail may not be from New Bank Online?

   _____

   _____

2. Identify two (2) things in the e-mail message that indicate that Andrew is the recipient of a phishing scam.

   _____

   _____

Surfers Beware

Privacy is becoming a major concern for everyone using the Internet. When you surf from one Web site to the next, the links and pages that you click on are tracked using cookies. In computer terms, a **cookie** is information that a computer receives and sends back to a Web site to track user visits and activity. Cookies are like a footprint pattern that lets everyone know where you have been on the Web. Many online retailers use cookies to track items in a shopping cart. Some Web sites use cookies to store login information. Many responsible Web sites will alert visitors that cookies are being used, but such a disclosure is not a requirement in the United States.

Cookies are great if you do not like going through the hassle of retyping the same information over and over again. However, if you do not want the prying eyes of Web site owners and advertisers looking into your browsing history, you may want to take action to restrict what cookies can and cannot do. Fortunately, you do have some control over what you want Web sites to record about your Internet activity. Cookies are stored in

Web browsers, and most cookie options can be found under the "Privacy" setting. The options menu will allow you to ban all cookies, making some Web sites difficult to navigate or inaccessible. Alternatively, you can curb the use of cookies at Web sites you do not visit often while allowing them at your favorite news, e-mail, and weather sites. The good news is that cookies cannot transfer viruses or malware to your computer, but some viruses and malware can be disguised as cookies.

In summary, remember that your movements online are being watched, but protecting your online privacy starts with you. By controlling cookies, using strong passwords, installing and using antivirus software, recognizing and deleting suspicious e-mails, and restricting what you share on social media sites, you can remain in the driver's seat and keep your personal information safe and secure.

Activity #4

Directions: Use the information in the passage to answer each question.

1. How are cookies like a footprint pattern?

_____

_____

2. What is a benefit of using cookies?

_____

_____

3. Where are cookies stored?

_____

_____

4. Certain free e-mail accounts use cookies to track Internet activity and personal information. Why are Web sites that offer free e-mail services not so free?

_____

_____

5. How can you protect your online safety?

_____

_____

Key Terms

Cookie	Information that a computer receives and sends back to a Web site to track user visits and activity.
Cybercriminal	A person who commits a computer-related crime.
Cyber Threat Actor	A fake entity that uses natural disasters and other high profile events to request financial assistance or spread malware.
Data Breach	An occurrence involving the viewing, theft, copying, transmission, or use of protected, confidential, or otherwise sensitive information by someone without permission to access such information.
Ethernet Cable	A computer cable that connects the computer to high speed Internet.
Hack	To change information on a computer system in order to access data illegally.
Hacker	Someone who tries to obtain unauthorized access to a computer in order to get information that can be used for personal gain.
Malware	A type of malicious software that harms a computer.
Phishing Scam	An attempt through electronic means to get confidential or personal information from someone in a dishonest way.
Product Key	A specialized code for licensed software that certifies that the copy of the program is original.
Unsecured Wireless Network	A computer network that permits access to the Internet without entering a password.

Introduction

Objectives – After completing this lesson, you will be able to:

- Kickstart your online job search
- Avoid job scams
- Discover your personality type using the Holland Codes
- Develop a professional profile
- Describe hardware and software requirements for taking an online course
- Debunk myths about taking courses online

Key Terms

- Elevator Speech
- Hashtag
- Holland Codes
- Learning Management System
- Personal Brand
- RIASEC
- Webinar

Job Search

If you are in the market for a new job or a career change, your computer skills coupled with a good job search plan can help you find a job that is right for you. Your computer skills will help you navigate various Web sites and use online tools more effectively. A good job search plan will give you focus so that you do not waste time pursuing the wrong opportunities. According to the Department of Labor, a typical job search can take up to ten months. With such a long process ahead of you, how do you get started?

It is important to begin the process by taking a good look at your current skills and interests and the types of jobs that will be a good fit based on who you are as a person. Applying for jobs that you are not qualified for or do not interest you will not be very good use of your time. Instead, it is important to start the job search process with an assessment of your interests. One tool that has been used to help job candidates make career choices that will land them in a happy and productive work environment is the RIASEC test. The RIASEC test is based on the Holland Codes, which is a theory developed by American psychologist John L. Holland. According to Holland's research, a person can thrive in a career environment that reflects their personality type. Holland developed six (6) types of personality to help individuals select careers that are a match with their personal traits. The six work personalities are as follows:

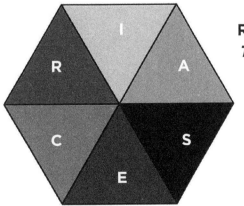

John L. Holland's RIASEC hexagon of *The Holland Codes*

Holland Code	Personality Type	Worker Profile
R	Realistic	Doers
I	Investigative	Thinkers
A	Artistic	Creators
S	Social	Helpers
E	Enterprising	Persuaders
C	Conventional	Organizers

Source: Making Vocational Choices by John Holland (3rd Edition) (1997)

Once you have identified your strengths and figured out what makes you tick as a person (see **Activity #1**), you can use the Internet to research job opportunities, salaries, and professional networks to help you build an effective job search campaign. Below are practical steps that you can take to put your job search campaign into action.

Job Search Campaign Action Plan

1) **Use employment sites to search for job openings.** See if your skills and qualifications match what employers are seeking.

    - Indeed.com
    - Simplyhired.com
    - Idealist.org (for nonprofit jobs)

2) **Find helpful resources on LinkedIn.** Use LinkedIn to connect to people you know and search for people who have a job similar to what you want to do. You can also join personal interest groups, participate in discussions, post a professional recommendation or article you have written on your page, search for opportunities, and receive career tips.

3) **Contact your network.** Let family, friends, supervisors, professors, and mentors know that you are looking for a job. Inquire about potential opportunities at their place of employment and ask for contacts.

4) **Research companies.** It is important to understand information about a company's products, services, values, mission, competitors, and overall business environment. Most employers will have a corporate Web site. Additionally, resources like Hoovers.com have information on over 85 million companies. The information available at company-focused Web sites will help you answer questions about why you are interested in working at a particular company and also help to determine whether a specific company is a good fit for you.

5) **Research salary information at Glassdoor.com.** Although salary is not the only factor when making a career decision, knowing an average salary or pay rate for your chosen career can shape your expectations about what you can realistically expect to earn. You can determine if a career, or related career path, will pay enough to meet your lifestyle needs.

6) **Follow up with all contacts.** Following up shows interest and is a great opportunity to receive advice as you apply for different jobs, learn more about what it is like to work for a particular organization, perfect your online profile (discussed later in this lesson), interview, and weigh various options.

7) **Beware of job scams.** Unfortunately, technology makes it easy for scammers to create fake job positions in an attempt to take advantage of job hunters. It is important to exercise common sense and caution when applying for jobs. See the red flags below to avoid being scammed.

12 Job Scam Red Flags

1) As the saying goes, if the job opportunity seems too good to be true, then it probably is.

2) There are numerous misspellings in the job description.

3) You are hired without an interview or meeting a representative from your potential employer.

4) You are asked to provide credit card or bank or PayPal account numbers.

5) Instead of mentioning the responsibilities of the position, the job posting focuses on the amount of money that will be made.

6) You are asked to send a payment by wire service (e.g., Western Union).

7) You are offered a large payment in exchange for allowing the use of your bank account – often for depositing checks or transferring money.

8) You receive a large check unexpectedly.

9) You are promised a large salary for very little work.

10) You are asked to provide sensitive information such as your Social Security number or a copy of your driver's license before being considered for the job.

11) You must complete a background check before you can be considered for the position.

12) You receive an e-mail from someone in the company, but the e-mail address doesn't match the company's Web site domain (e.g., jdoe@gmail.com instead of jdoe@companyname.com).

The R.E.E.L.

The
R.E.E.L.

Real Experiences
in Everyday Life

Cybercriminals are often able to con job seekers out of money using a check scam. Read the scenario below and answer the question that follows.

Beth

Scenario: Beth has applied for a position with Company ABC that appears too good to be true. She has a telephone interview with a representative from the company and is told that she will receive a salary that seems way above the range for the entry-level position that she has applied. Three days after her interview she receives a large check in the mail unexpectedly from Company ABC. The check is enclosed in a letter that tells her that she will be offered a position pending her ability to follow the instructions outlined in the letter. Beth notices some typos in the letter, but doesn't think much of them. The instructions direct Beth to deposit the check into her bank account and quickly forward a portion of the funds to the Operations Director (Mr. Ted Manning) using Western Union. Beth does as instructed. The next business day, Beth checks her bank account online and notices that the check she received from Company ABC bounced. The money she wired was actually her own money and there is no way to trace or recover the funds.

What job scam red flags did Beth ignore?

_____

_____

_____

_____

The RIASEC TEST – Discover Your Interests!
Adapted from Holland Codes, Wikipedia

1) **Directions:** Read each statement. If you agree with the statement, fill in the circle. There are no wrong answers.

	Statement	R	I	A	S	E	C
1)	I like to use tools.	●					
2)	I like to discover new things.		●				
3)	I like to draw.			●			
4)	I like helping others.				●		
5)	I would like to start my own own business.					●	
6)	I like working with numbers.						●
7)	I like to build things.	●					
8)	I like visiting art museums.			●			
9)	I like to follow the rules.						●
10)	I like to influence others.					●	
11)	I like to do research.		●				
12)	I like donating to charities.				●		
13)	I like to teach others.				●		
14)	I enjoy being outdoors.	●					
15)	I prefer to work at an organized desk.						●
16)	I like speaking before an audience.					●	
17)	I enjoy playing a musical instrument.			●			
18)	I like science.		●				
19)	I enjoy leading others.					●	
20)	I encourage others to go vote in major elections.				●		
21)	I like to solve mysteries.		●				
TOTAL:							
		R	I	A	S	E	C

	Statement	R	I	A	S	E	C
22)	I like to have a garden.	●					
23)	I like decorating.			●			
24)	I pay attention to details.						●
25)	I like to analyze problems.		●				
26)	I like creating procedures for doing things.						●
27)	I enjoy singing in a choir.			●			
28)	I like having a budget for household expenses.	●					
29)	I set goals for myself.					●	
30)	I have good taste in fashion.			●			
31)	I am good at sports.	●					
32)	I like reading charts & graphs.		●				
33)	I like to cook.	●					
34)	I like to work in teams.				●		
35)	I'm good at keeping tax records.						●
36)	I am competitive.					●	
37)	I like to volunteer in my community.				●		
38)	I like to work in an office.						●
39)	I like asking questions.		●				
40)	I enjoy learning new dances.			●			
41)	I like learing about other cultures.			●			
42)	I am not afraid of taking risks.					●	
TOTAL:							
		R	I	A	S	E	C

R	I	A	S	E	C

2) **Directions:** Add up the number of filled in circles in each column and then add the two columns together for a grand total.

RIASEC TEST Results

Directions: Take the three letters with the highest scores and record them under "My Interest Code." Then refer to the table to see what your "Interest Code" means.

MY INTEREST CODE

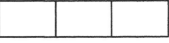

R = Realistic

Realistic people, or doers, are no-nonsense, down-to-earth people. They enjoy mechanical or athletic jobs, and like working with their hands.

Career fields include the following:
- Engineering
- Construction
- Information Technology/ Computers
- Advanced Manufacturing
- Food and Hospitality
- Agriculture

I = Investigative

Investigative people, or thinkers, like to watch, learn, analyze, and solve problems.

Career fields include the following:
- Biotechnology
- Chemistry
- Big Data Analytics
- Medicine/Surgery
- Economics
- Cyber Security

A = Artistic

Artistic people, or creators, like to work in unstructured environments where they can be free to innovate.

Career fields include the following:
- Fine and Performing Arts
- Broadcast Journalism
- Architecture
- Interior Design
- Photography
- Cosmetology

S = Social

Social people, or helpers, are cooperative, caring, and enjoy working with others.

Career fields include the following:
- Nursing
- Counseling
- Education
- Public Relations
- Customer Service
- Social Work

E = Enterprising

Enterprising people, or persuaders, are ambitious, energetic, and confident. They like leadership roles and prefer work that is competitive in nature.

Career fields include the following:
- Sales/Marketing
- Law
- Real Estate
- Politics
- Banking/Finance
- Entrepreneurship

C = Conventional

Conventional people, or organizers, are detail-oriented, thorough, and organized. They excel in structured environments and office settings.

Career fields include the following:
- Accounting
- Insurance
- Administration
- Data Processing
- Library Science
- Asset Management

Creating a Professional Profile

Having a professional profile is one way to communicate your interests and skills beyond what someone may read on a resume. The Internet has made it relatively easy to give employers, associates, mentors, and other people in your professional circle a better picture of what makes you unique. Your profile should start with an introductory statement of who you are and what drives you. You should include examples of experiences and skills that reinforce your key attributes. Think of this brief introduction as your written elevator speech. An **elevator speech** is simply a brief message about who you are, what you hope to achieve, and how you can benefit an organization. It is about thirty (30) seconds and can also encourage interest in a project, idea, or product.

Sample Elevator Speeches

Profile Type	Speech
Job Seeker	*"I have a passion for helping others solve their problems. I have been serving students at the collegiate level for over five years and recently was an August 2017 Service Award Recipient for providing outstanding service for the Office of Student Affairs at ABC University. I like the challenge of responding to customers' increasing expectations and look forward to building value, loyalty, and trust with the people I serve."*
Entrepreneur	*"I am a Web site analyst. I study the traffic of your Web site and find out where your Web site is leaving money on the table and how it can better attract and engage your customers. Web site data doesn't reveal why people do what they do at your Web site, but it does reveal the story of what they do and how they do it. This is an important and interesting story for your business to understand, and I want to share this story with you."*

Once you have perfected your elevator speech, you can enhance your profile with links to articles that you have written, positive press you have received, videos you directed, a Web site that you coded and designed, recommendations highlighting your strengths, and any other information that provides insights on your accomplishments and ability to add value. It is also important to have a picture that reflects your **personal brand**. Your personal brand is the impression about you that you want to create in the minds of others. This picture can be a casual photo or an image showcasing you in business attire. Whichever photo you choose, it should be appropriate and consistently displayed across social media platforms so that others can recognize who you are.

Now that you have perfected your profile, it is time to make this profile available for others to see. There are several Web sites that can help you network and build an online presence. Listed below are a few of these Web sites along with tips to ensure that your professional profile gets noticed.

Facebook

- Join industry and alumni groups to connect with others.
- Post interesting content that relates to fields that are relevant to you. Discuss this content with peers. For example, that podcast you saw on how to buy your first rental property could create a great discussion for you and your buddies looking to invest in real estate.

Twitter

- Follow companies and people that interest you.
- Get feedback and opinions from your followers.
- Use hashtags. A **hashtag** is a word or phrase, preceded by a hash mark (#), used within a message to identify a keyword or topic of interest and facilitate a search for it.

LinkedIn

- Add connections to people you know.
- Highlight your skills and accomplishments.
- Request recommendations.
- Search for job opportunities.

Pinterest

- Pin pictures related to your experiences.
- Explore company pins and follow employers you wish to work for.
- Create a portfolio board that highlights examples of your work.

Activity #2

Directions: Answer each question.

1. Write an elevator speech for yourself. Practice saying this speech with another person. How can you improve your elevator speech?

   _____

   _____

   _____

   _____

2. If a job recruiter were to Google your name, what three things would you like for him or her to learn about you?

   a) _____

   b) _____

   c) _____

3. Name two groups that you would join on Facebook? What does each group reveal about you?

   a) _____

   b) _____

4. Name two companies that you would follow on Twitter. Why would you follow each company?

   a) _____

   b) _____

Taking Courses Online

Taking a course online is not as easy as it sounds. It is true that you do not have to be in a physical building and you can generally access a course when and where you want, but there are requirements to be successful. First of all, the hardware and software on your computer must be compatible with the learning management system that houses the course. A **learning management system**, or LMS, is software used to deliver an educational course or training program. Popular LMSs include Blackboard, Moodle, Canvas, and Sakai. Most colleges providing online courses will outline the hardware and software specifications. Additionally, there will be online tutorials or a **webinar** for using a particular LMS effectively. A webinar is a meeting or presentation conducted over the Internet where participants can ask questions and interact with the presenter.

You can expect technical requirements for an online class to include the following:

- Windows or Mac-based computer (tablets, smartphones, and other mobile devices are usually not sufficient)
- Recent operating system running on your computer
- Reliable, high-speed Internet access
- Internet browser that is supported by the program

Far too many students become bogged down with technical problems that prevent them from finishing their work. Thus, test your computer early on to ensure that you can access and use all coursework. If something is not working correctly, reach out to the technical support hotline so that issues can be resolved before classes begin.

Having the right hardware and software is not enough to succeed in an online class. Taking a course online requires discipline, time management, and a good workspace. It is easy to fall behind because a full-semester's worth of content is covered in half the time, doubling the pace of the course. In addition to the fast pace, the unstructured nature of an online course means that you have to carve out blocks of time in your schedule to complete assignments and interact with your professor and classmates. Becoming distracted, disengaged, or too busy with other responsibilities makes it more difficult to fulfill commitments related to the online course. Thus, it is easy to walk away and quit. If you feel like giving up, reach out to your professor, counselor, or success coach assigned to you. You are paying for these resources, so be sure to use them.

Many studies have concluded that some learners need to be in a face-to-face classroom in order to retain and apply instructional materials. Thus, it is important to know the type of learner you are and have the right expectations about taking a course online from the start. If you determine that you can learn in a virtual environment, be prepared, keep a close eye on assignment due dates, and use the convenience factor to your advantage.

Activity #3

Directions: Read each statement about taking courses online and decide whether you agree or disagree with it. Circle your answer.

1. A benefit of taking an online course is that you can take as long as you want to complete the course.

   Agree   Disagree

2. Online courses have the same rigor and expectations as face-to-face courses.

   Agree   Disagree

3. You have support from many sources when you take an online class.

   Agree   Disagree

4. If you enroll in an online course, you will be taught how to use a computer.

   Agree   Disagree

5. Online courses demand engagement and a high level of involvement.

   Agree   Disagree

6. Most online classes require students to log-on only once during a given week.

   Agree   Disagree

7. Studies indicate that students who succeed in online courses tend to procrastinate.

   Agree   Disagree

8. Employers do not accept online degrees.

   Agree   Disagree

Key Terms

Elevator Speech

A brief message about who you are, what you hope to achieve, and how you can benefit an organization.

Hashtag

A word or phrase, preceded by a hash mark (#), used within a message to identify a keyword or topic of interest and facilitate a search for it.

Holland Codes

A theory developed by American psychologist John L. Holland that links personality types to the world of work. According to Holland's research, a person can thrive in a career environment that reflects their personality type.

Learning Management System (LMS)

Software used to deliver an educational course or training program.

Personal Brand

An impression that is formed based on someone's online and offline presence.

RIASEC

John Holland's six (6) types of personality. The abbreviation stands for Realistic, Investigative, Artistic, Social, Enterprising, and Conventional.

Webinar

A meeting or presentation conducted over the Internet where participants can ask questions and interact with the presenter.

Computers: One Click at a Time

ANSWER KEYS

Activity #1

Directions: It's time to check your understanding of the background of computers. Read each question. Circle the **best** answer.

1. According to Chart 1, what percentage of U.S. households owned a computer in 1993?

    A) 61.8%

    B) 84%

    C) 22.9%

2. Based on the passage, what is meant by the **widespread** use of computers?

    A) Computers can be found in every country in the world.

    B) Computers are used by many different people for a variety of purposes.

    C) Computers are so large that they can cover an entire desk.

3. Leisure can be defined as **free time to do something that you enjoy**. According to the passage, we rely on computers for leisure activities. Which one of the following activities is most likely to be a leisure activity made possible by the use of computers?

    A) writing a resume

    B) cleaning the house

    C) listening to music

4. A decade is a **period of ten years**. Referring to Chart 1, approximately how many decades are between 1984 and 2013?

    A) three

    B) four

    C) two

5. **True** or **False**. Write **T** for True or **F** for False next to the statements below.

    F a) In the early 1970s many people began purchasing computers for personal use in the home.

    Explanation: This statement is false. Up until the late 1970s or early 1980s, computers were mostly used by large corporations and governments.

T b) According to Chart 1, computer ownership by American households more than doubled from 1993 to 2003.

Explanation: *This statement is true. Computer use from 1993 to 2003 increased from 22.9% to 61.8%. 22.9% doubled, or times 2, is 45.8%. 61.8% is greater than 45.8% (i.e., more than double). Also, comparing the size of the bar in 1993 to the size of the bar in 2003 would allow you to reach the same conclusion with an "eyeball" view.*

The R.E.E.L.

Directions: Look at each picture in the left column. Use the space in the right column to describe briefly how the use of a computer (or a computer program) is solving a problem or making life easier or more enjoyable.

Picture	What role does the computer play?
GPS	Obtaining directions and viewing maps is now paperless and more convenient with an in-car navigation system, or GPS. Answers will vary.
(email icon)	Delivery of messages to friends and loved ones doesn't have to take days...it's now instantaneous thanks to e-mail. Answers will vary.
(game console)	People can play video games with players in multiple locations. Answers will vary.
(X-rays)	Doctors can view X-rays immediately on a computer screen. Answers will vary.
(smartphone)	Smartphones perform many functions, but for a simple task like calling others, communicating can take place anywhere that has a good connection. Answers will vary.
SLOT MACHINE	A computer generates random numbers and symbols to make casino gaming experiences fun and unpredictable. Answers will vary.

Purchasing a Computer Introduction

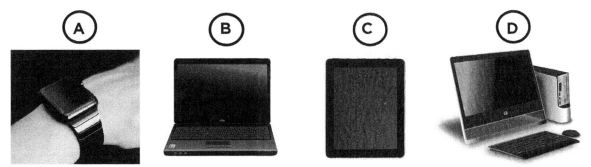

How many items did you circle? **All items should be circled.** Can you identify each device? Write your answers below.

A _Smartwatch or Wearable Device_

B _Laptop_

C _Tablet_

D _Desktop_

Activity #2

Directions: Your job is to help Pam, Sergio, Robert, and Selina purchase a computer. They each have different needs and want a computer that will fit their lifestyle. Read each description of the different types of computers. Then, read the comments made by Pam, Sergio, Robert, and Selina and use these comments to select the best computer that will fit their needs.

Computer Buyer	Comments	Best Computer?
1) Pam	"I need a small device that I can take with me during my morning walks. The device needs to track my number of steps, calories burned, and heart rate."	Smartwatch or Wearable Device
2) Sergio	"I need a small computer that I can take with me when I study in the library."	Laptop
3) Robert	"I need a computer that I can keep on my desk in my office. It needs to have a wide screen and keys large enough for my big fingers."	Desktop
4) Selina	"I need a computer that I can take with me when I travel on vacation. I will mainly use it to read eBooks, so having a touchscreen interface is important to me."	Tablet

Activity #3

Directions: It's now time to test your knowledge of computer parts. Take a few moments to review the **hardware** below. Then, select the name from the parts list that best identifies the part and write that name next to the corresponding number in the table. Also, indicate whether the part is an **input** or **output** part, if applicable.

	Computer Part	"Input" or "Output"
1	Monitor	Output
2	Printer	Output
3	Webcam	Input
4	Mouse	Input
5	Tower	N/A
6	Wireless Mouse	Input
7	Touchpad	Input
8	Keyboard	Input

1

2

3

4

5

6

7

8

Activity #4

Directions: Now that you can identify the main parts of a computer, it's important to understand what each part does. Draw a line to match the computer part with the best description. Feel free to refer to the pictures in Activity #3 if you need help.

Computer Part	Description

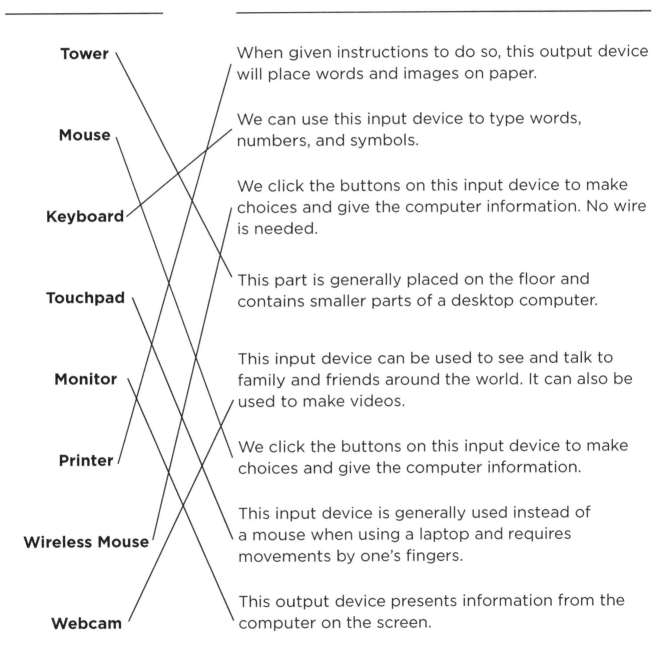

Tower

Mouse

Keyboard

Touchpad

Monitor

Printer

Wireless Mouse

Webcam

When given instructions to do so, this output device will place words and images on paper.

We can use this input device to type words, numbers, and symbols.

We click the buttons on this input device to make choices and give the computer information. No wire is needed.

This part is generally placed on the floor and contains smaller parts of a desktop computer.

This input device can be used to see and talk to family and friends around the world. It can also be used to make videos.

We click the buttons on this input device to make choices and give the computer information.

This input device is generally used instead of a mouse when using a laptop and requires movements by one's fingers.

This output device presents information from the computer on the screen.

Activity #5

Directions: Read each question. Circle the **best** answer.

1. Circle the image that best represents the power button on a computer.

2. Based on the passage, what is the best way to turn off your computer?

    A) Press the power button

    B) Unplug the computer's power supply

    C) Go to the start button located on your screen and select "shut down," "hibernate," or "sleep"

3. **True** or **False**. Write **T** for True or **F** for False next to the statements below.

    T a) In sleep mode, the computer is not completely turned off.

    Explanation: *This statement is true. In sleep mode, the computer enters a low-power state.*

    F b) In hibernate mode you can return to your open sessions later.

    Explanation: *This statement is false. In sleep mode you can return to your open sessions later.*

Activity #6

Directions: Consider each task below numbered one (1) through ten (10). Refer to the list of ten keyboard keys and write the name of the key that would best accomplish the task listed in the left column of the table.

Task	Keyboard Key
1) Put a space between words or letters	Space Bar
2) Erase the letter to the right of the cursor	Delete
3) Capitalize the first letter of a person's name	Shift
4) Move the cursor down to the next line	Enter
5) Put five spaces at the beginning of a paragraph	Tab
6) Move to the beginning of the line	Home
7) Move up the screen several lines at a time	Page Up
8) Remove a sentence that you just typed by moving backwards	Backspace
9) Capitalize an entire sentence for emphasis	Caps Lock
10) Go to the end of the line	End

The R.E.E.L.

Directions: Which printer would you choose for the following workloads? Circle your answer.

- Family photos — (inkjet) or laser printer
- Heavy volumes of text-based documents — inkjet or (laser printer)
- Small school projects — (inkjet) or laser printer

Activity #1

Directions: Each letter represents a specific area of the computer. Read each question and circle the **best** answer based on the information in the passage about "The Desktop."

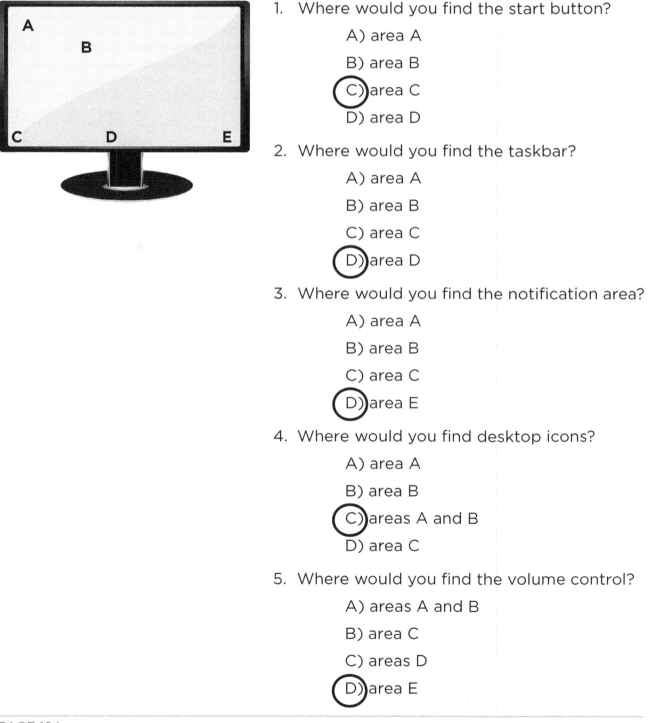

1. Where would you find the start button?

    A) area A

    B) area B

    C) area C

    D) area D

2. Where would you find the taskbar?

    A) area A

    B) area B

    C) area C

    D) area D

3. Where would you find the notification area?

    A) area A

    B) area B

    C) area C

    D) area E

4. Where would you find desktop icons?

    A) area A

    B) area B

    C) areas A and B

    D) area C

5. Where would you find the volume control?

    A) areas A and B

    B) area C

    C) areas D

    D) area E

Activity #2

Directions: Read each question. Provide the **best** answer(s).

1. Which button allows you to hide a window?

    A) restore down

    (B) minimize

    C) maximize

2. Which button allows you to make a window larger and fill the screen?

    A) close

    (B) maximize

    C) restore down

3. Which bar shows the name of the folder, document, or program that you are using?

    A) taskbar

    B) scroll bar

    (C) title bar

4. Provide at least two (2) ways that you will know that a program that is open on your computer screen is active and ready for your use.

    1) There will be a highlighted title bar indicating an active window.

    2) The program will appear in a window that is in front of other windows.

    3) The corresponding button of the open program on the taskbar will be a different color compared to the other buttons.

    Answers will vary

5. Based on what you have learned thus far in the first two lessons of this book, identify four ways that you can move up and down a Web page that is too large to fit on one screen.

    1) Use the scroll bar.

    2) Use the up and down arrows on the keyboard to scroll.

    3) Use the PageUp and PageDown keys on the keyboard.

    4) Use the scroll wheel on your mouse.

    Answers will vary

Activity #1

Directions: Read each question and provide the **best** answer(s).

1. If you were to purchase an HP (Hewlett Packard) desktop, which operating system would you expect to find running on your machine?

    A) Chrome OS

    B) Microsoft Windows

    C) macOS

    D) Linux

    E) Tizen

2. If you were to purchase a MacBook Pro, which operating system would you expect to find running on your machine?

    A) Chrome OS

    B) Microsoft Windows

    C) macOS

    D) Linux

    E) Tizen

3. If you were to purchase a Lenovo ThinkPad, which operating system would you expect to find running on your machine?

    A) Chrome OS

    B) Microsoft Windows

    C) macOS

    D) Linux

    E) Tizen

4. If you were to purchase a Samsung smart TV, which operating system would you expect to find running on your television?

    A) Chrome OS

    B) Microsoft Windows

    C) macOS

    D) Linux

    E) Tizen

5. The "Smart Home" image below presents icons of several items in a smart home that could be powered by an operating system. Can you list five of these items?

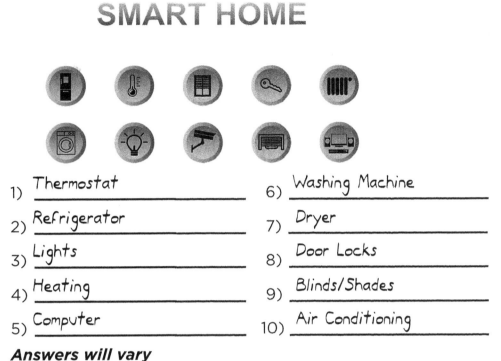

SMART HOME

1) Thermostat
2) Refrigerator
3) Lights
4) Heating
5) Computer

6) Washing Machine
7) Dryer
8) Door Locks
9) Blinds/Shades
10) Air Conditioning

Answers will vary

6. Referring back to Question #5 and the "Smart Home" illustration, what other "smart" items might be found in the home that are not represented in the image? Name at least two.

Television	Security Devices	Oven
Faucet	Water Heater	Toilet

Answers will vary

7. Street cameras are often used by police and law enforcement agencies to improve roadway safety while capturing important information. Many street cameras employ a state of the art operating system that allows many value-added applications to occur. Read the list of applications. For each application, suggest a problem that is being solved

Application

1) Cameras track when and where a vehicle enters and exits a toll road.

What problem is being solved?

Less staff is needed to operate tollbooths and drivers save time by avoiding having to pay road usage fees while traveling. *Answers will vary*

Application	What problem is being solved?
2) Cameras measure a vehicle's speed.	Law enforcement can enforce speed limit guidelines and monitor traffic patterns. *Answers will vary*
3) In a parking lot, cameras store the license plate of vehicles along with the parking ticket number.	Car theft can be prevented because the exit barrier can be programmed to open only if the parking ticket presented matches the license plate. *Answers will vary*
4) Cameras monitor the vehicles coming to and leaving a major sporting event.	Security can be maintained. *Answers will vary*
5) Cameras identify hazardous goods being transported through a tunnel.	In the event of an emergency, officials will know what precautions to take for overall safety. *Answers will vary*

The R.E.E.L.

Can you tell which mobile operating system is running each mobile device below? (Hint: For the two smartphones, look at how each phone is designed and determine the manufacturer.)

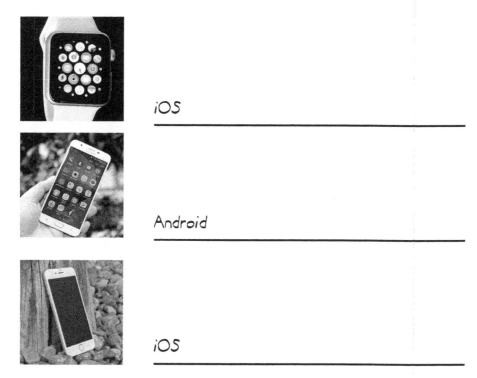

iOS

Android

iOS

Activity #2

Directions: You have just been given a document to format using Microsoft Word. However, before you can make the necessary changes to the document in an efficient manner, you must understand the purpose of commonly used sssing symbols. For each icon below, write its purpose. (Hint: Use the pictures to help you, as the purpose is closely related to the look of the icon.)

Icon	Purpose
B	To make text **bold**
I	To put text in *italics* format
U	To underline text
ABC ✓	To check spelling and grammar
☰	To center text
☰	To align text to the left
⋮≡	To create bullets for text
🔍🖨	To preview a document before printing
↶	To undo typing
A	To change the font in terms of design, style, size, color, and/or effects

Activity #3

Directions: Figure 3-2 provides financial information for Candy Café over a six-month period. Review the information and answer the questions that follow, using your knowledge of spreadsheets.

Figure 3-2: Candy Café Financial Information

	A	B	C	D	E	F	G	E
1		January	February	March	April	May	June	Total
2	Sales	$21,000	$22,000	$23,000	$23,500	$24,000	$25,000	**$138,500**
3	Expenses	$20,900	$21,100	$21,900	$22,200	$22,700	$23,100	**$131,900**
4	Profits	$100	$900		$1,300	$1,300	$1,900	
5								

Note: Sales - Expenses = Profits

1. In what cell will you find sales for the month of February?

   _____C2_____

2. In what cell will you find profits for the month of May?

   _____F4_____

3. What month is in cell D1?

   _____March_____

4. What range of cells represents expenses for January through June?

   _____B3:G3_____

5. Using cell references, write a formula that expresses the value of profits for the month of March. _____=D2-D3_____

6. How much profit was earned in March?

   _____$1,100_____

7. Using the SUM function, write a formula to express the value of total sales for January through June. _____=SUM(B2:G2)_____

8. Using cell references, write a formula to determine the total profits for January through June.

   =E2-E3 or
   =SUM(B4:G4) or
   =B4+C4+D4+E4+F4+G4

9. Using the value you found in #6, what are the total profits for January through June?

   _____$6,600_____

Activity #4

Directions: Read each scenario. Provide the **best** answer.

1. Anna clicked on a link she received via e-mail from what appeared to be a legitimate delivery company. She expected to receive tracking information on a package. Instead, when she clicked on the link, her computer locked and she couldn't type anything using her keyboard. A message appeared demanding that she go to her nearest Wal-Mart and wire $1500 to an unknown recipient in order to be able to use her computer again and have access to her files. What sort of threat is Anna experiencing??

    A) a virus

    B) spyware

    C) ransomware

2. Bobby returned to work after taking a brief lunch break. To his surprise, one of his co-workers received a deceptive program that spread from her computer to every computer in the office. Bobby's computer was infected and he could not finish his work. What sort of threat is Bobby experiencing?

    A) a virus

    B) spyware

    C) ransomware

3. Jennifer is used to seeing annoying pop-up ads appear when she is using Google Chrome as her Web browser. Usually, there is some type of product being advertised. Today, however, she receives a pop-up ad with a message that says that her computer is about to crash. No matter what she does, the pop-up ad will not go away. What sort of threat is Jennifer experiencing?

    A) a virus

    B) malware

    C) ransomware

4. Jill has noticed that every time she surfs the Internet, banner advertisements appear that reflect her Web surfing habits. She feels like she's being watched. What sort of threat is Jill experiencing?

    A) adware

    B) spyware

    C) ransomware

    D) a virus

    E) both A and B *(adware is a form of spyware)*

5. Victor got a great deal on a popular antivirus software program released in 2015. The program received great reviews when it first became available for consumers to purchase. Victor installed the program on his computer. What mistake did Victor make in purchasing the software?

Victor did not buy the most up-to-date version of the antivirus software.

An older version may not be able to handle the latest attacks and threats.

Answers will vary

Activity #1

Directions: Read each question and provide the **best** answer.

1. Based on what you have learned about shopping online, which online retailer would be the best place to buy office supplies?

   A) Sam's Office Shack

   B) Office Depot

   C) Home Goods

2. What information appearing in the address bar indicates that the Web site is secure?

   A) http://

   B) ssl://

   C) https://

3. Which information is not needed during the checkout process?

   A) date of birth

   B) billing address

   C) credit card number

4. It's time to shop online! Number the following seven (7) steps in the correct order, with one (1) being the first step and seven (7) being the final step.

Step	Order (1 to 7)
Click the checkout button	2
Track your package	6
Submit your order	4
Receive your merchandise	7
Add items to your shopping cart	1
Receive an order confirmation via e-mail	5
Enter the shipping address and your credit card information	3

Activity #2

Directions: Below are sample security questions, many of which are used for password resets. Answer each question, noting whether **simple**, **memorable**, **stable**, **multiple**, and **safe** (S-M-S-M-S) applies to the question and your answer. Circle the S-M-S-M-S characteristics that apply.

Answers will vary

Activity #3

Directions: Read each question and provide the **best** answer.

1. Based on the statistics provided in the reading, which social media site is known to be highly popular with young adults (i.e., 18-29 year olds)?

    A) LinkedIn

    B) Facebook

    C) Twitter

    D) Instagram

2. Based on the statistics provided in the reading, which social media site is known to be popular with college graduates?

    A) Twitter

    B) LinkedIn

    C) Facebook

    D) Pinterest

3. On which social media site are you likely to tweet about current events?

    A) YouTube

    B) Pinterest

    C) Twitter

    D) Instagram

4. Which social media networking site is the most widely-used among all age groups?

    A) Pinterest

    B) LinkedIn

    C) YouTube

    D) Facebook

5. Which social media site is often referred to as a business social network?
   - A) LinkedIn
   - B) Pinterest
   - C) Twitter
   - D) Instagram

6. When using social media, why is it important to keep your digital life separate from your personal life?

   Sharing too much personal information can fuel cybercriminals. Also, revealing personal problems to a world audience can affect your reputation and could turn-off a potential employer.

   Answers will vary

7. When using social media, why is it important <u>not</u> to trust too easily?

   Much of what you see, read, and hear is not true. Also, fake news tends to spread quickly.

   Answers will vary

Activity #1

Directions: It's time to check your understanding of an e-mail address. Read each question. Circle the **best** answer.

1. Which of the following symbols represents the "at" symbol?

    A) #

    B) &

    (C) @

2. Which of the following is not a main part of an e-mail address?

    (A) the password

    B) the username

    C) the domain

3. Which of the following is an example of a valid e-mail address?

    A) johnsmith@nyc.gov

    B) scorpio22@gmail.com

    C) pjones@californiacolleges.edu

    (D) All of the above

4. **True** or **False**. Write **T** for True or **F** for False next to the statements below.

    F   a) It is possible to have the same e-mail address as a relative who shares your last name.

    > **Explanation:** *Both the sender and the recipient must have an e-mail address that no one else has.*

    T   b) You can have more than one e-mail address.

    > **Explanation:** *Having more than one e-mail address is very common. Many people have a professional e-mail address for their place of work and a separate e-mail address for personal use.*

    F   c) It is not possible to have an e-mail address that ends in ".org".

    > **Explanation:** *The domain ".org" is short for organization and is a very common domain name. In fact, many nonprofit organizations have a ".org" domain name.*

Activity #2

Directions: Maria has chosen to open a free e-mail account using Google Mail, or Gmail. Initially, however, Maria makes a few mistakes. Read each scenario and provide a response that would help Maria with the correct use of e-mail.

Scenario 1:

Maria chooses a username for herself that's exactly the same as her cousin Stella's. What should Maria have done differently?

Maria's e-mail address will not be valid. She should have chosen a unique e-mail address.

Answers will vary

Scenario 2:

Maria is completely set up and has a valid e-mail address. She sends a test e-mail to her best friend Patty. After sending the e-mail to Patty, she looks for a copy of that e-mail in her inbox.

What should Maria have done differently?

Maria should have looked for a copy of her e-mail to Patty in the "Sent" folder.

Answers will vary

Scenario 3:

Maria has received a response back from Patty. She immediately responds to Patty's e-mail by clicking on the "Forward" button.

What should Maria have done differently?

In order to respond to Patty without typing a new e-mail, Maria should have clicked on the "Reply" button.

Answers will vary

Scenario 4:

Maria wants to draft a new e-mail to her Uncle Chuck about an upcoming family reunion. She clicks on the "Send" button to draft the e-mail.

What should Maria have done differently?

Maria should have clicked on the "New Mail" button or a similar option such as "Compose" or "Write."

Answers will vary

Scenario 5:

Maria begins drafting her e-mail message to her Uncle Chuck. She types "Family Reunion" in the subject field and types her letter in the message field. She clicks "Send," but an error message appears saying that the e-mail cannot be sent.

What should Maria have done differently?

Maria should have typed her uncle's e-mail address in the "To" field or selected it from her "Contacts" folder.

Answers will vary

Activity #3

Directions: Assume that you have typed a valid e-mail address in the "To" field for someone you would like to send an e-mail attachment. Correctly order the following steps for attaching an e-mail attachment from one (1) to five (5) with one being the first step and five being the last step.

Step	Order (1 to 5)
Click "Send"	5
Select the file you want to include in the e-mail	3
Click "OK" or "Open"	4
Find the file you want to include in the e-mail	2
Click on the "Attach File" button or paperclip symbol	1

Activity #4

Directions: Read each statement about using e-mail folders and decide whether you agree or disagree with it. Circle your answer.

1. The "Junk E-mail" folder can contain both spam e-mails and legitimate e-mails.

    Agree   Disagree

   Explanation: *This is a true statement. Sometimes legitimate e-mails are routed to the "Junk" folder.*

2. The "Drafts" folder stores the e-mail addresses and contact information of family, friends, and colleagues.

Agree Disagree

Explanation: *The "Contacts" folder stores the e-mail addresses and contact information of family, friends, and colleagues.*

3. You should be very cautious of spam e-mails and e-mails from people you don't know.

 Agree   Disagree

Explanation: *This is a true statement. Many times the sender of spam e-mail is an advertiser, but sometimes the sender is someone who is trying to access information on your computer without your permission.*

4. When you delete an e-mail in your inbox, it is permanently removed from your electronic mailbox.

Agree 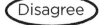 Disagree

Explanation: *When you delete an e-mail in your inbox, a copy of the e-mail is stored in the "Deleted Items" folder in case you need to access the e-mail message again.*

5. If you start an e-mail and want to finish it later, you can save it and come back to it at another time.

Agree   Disagree

Explanation: *This is a true statement. The "Drafts" folder will save a copy of e-mail messages that you start, but never finish or send. To finish an e-mail that was never sent, but saved, access the "Drafts" folder and select the e-mail that you saved.*

Activity #1

Directions: Read each question. Circle the **best** answer.

1. Which of the following is not a sign that your computer is being hacked?

    A) Your computer is doing things by itself.

    B) Your antivirus software turns off by itself.

    C) It takes a few minutes to download the latest antivirus program.

    D) Your computer runs unusually slow.

2. Hackers can make a great sum of money selling which of the following items about you?

    A) your address

    B) your home telephone number

    C) your e-mail address

    D) your medical records

3. If you are a victim of identity theft, which of the following entities will create an Identity Theft Report and recovery plan for you?

    A) Equifax

    B) Federal Trade Commission

    C) Transunion

    D) Experian

4. Which of the following is a corrective course of action to protect your identity?

    A) close new accounts opened in your name

    B) request a free copy of your credit report

    C) delete all the files on your computer

    D) only visit mysterious Web sites when you are on a computer at your local library

5. **True** or **False**. Write **T** for True or **F** for False next to the statements below.

 a) You should open an e-mail attachment if you are 75% certain of where it came from.

Explanation: *You should be absolutely certain (125% sure) of where the e-mail came from and that it is a legitimate e-mail before opening an e-mail attachment.*

 b) It is okay to share personal information on your hotel's Wi-Fi network.

Explanation: *Even at the big chains or most expensive hotels, it is difficult to know if the public Wi-Fi network is secure. Therefore, assume that it is not and do not share personal information while using the Wi-Fi connection.*

 c) You will always know when malware has invaded your computer system.

Explanation: *Some hackers and cybercriminals are so cunning that victims are not aware that their computer system is being illegally accessed or infected with malware.*

6. Tyler can't download the latest antivirus program and his computer all of sudden freezes. He suspects that his computer has been hacked and needs to protect it from any further damage. What should he do? Plan a course of action for Tyler using the steps below. Correctly order each step from one (1) to seven (7) with one being the first step and seven being the last step.

Step	Order (1 to 7)
Shut down the computer	2
Reinstall all software	6
Take the computer to a trusted repair shop	3
Scan all backup files for viruses	7
Wipe the hard drive clean	4
Pull the network cable on the computer	1
Reload the operating system	5

Activity #2

1. The list below contains twelve (12) potential passwords. Circle the **strong** passwords using the information you have learned about creating a secure password.

987654321=   Password1   #71Dwq83Pfn   starwars

bw?39P7dxp   flower   baseball   Trustno1

dragon   mZ26=f391B   princess   s94U$G593h

2. Creating a strong password that you can easily remember can be difficult. Some people think of a phrase or sentence and change that phrase or sentence into letters, numbers, and symbols in order to form a strong password. For example, "**Emily, for you I'd go to jail**" can be transformed into **MLE,4uIdgo2jl**. Read each sentence below aloud, paying close attention to the sounds made. Make a strong password using the sounds that you hear.

a) I'd hate to go for you

Idh82go4u

b) You are wonderful too!

URldrful2

c) Do you know anyone?

DoUnonel?

d) I see a canine cutie for me!

ICaK9qT4me

Answers will vary

Activity #3

Directions: Carefully review the suspicious e-mail referenced in **Figure 6-2** and answer the questions that follow.

1. What information in the sender's e-mail address is a red flag that the e-mail may not be from New Bank Online?

   Instead of having a .com domain, the e-mail address has a .tw domain, indicating that the e-mail was sent by someone in Taiwan.

2. Identify two (2) things in the e-mail message that indicate that Andrew is the recipient of a phishing scam.

   E-mail Message: *You have 1 ONLINE account update, Use the proceed link to update your Profile to enable us add secure Authentication.*

   The e-mail message itself is full of errors. In the first line, instead of having a period after the first sentence, there is a comma. Instead of saying "following link" the messages says "proceed link." The author seems to confuse preceding with proceed. Also, the second line is missing the word "to" between "us" and "add." Keep in mind that many cybercriminals residing in countries where English is not their native language will have poor grammar and spelling skills.

   Answers will vary

Activity #4

Directions: Use the information in the passage to answer each question.

1. How are cookies like a footprint pattern?

   Cookies track where you go on the Web. Web site owners are able to follow your cyber path (i.e., your every move). Also, just as a person's footprint serves as a unique identifier, each computer has a unique Internet Protocol (IP) address that identifies each computer using the Internet. Thus, there's no hiding when you're on the World Wide Web.

   ___

   Answers will vary

2. What is a benefit of using cookies?

   When shopping online, items in a shopping cart can be stored. Also, cookies remember usernames and passwords so that you don't have to retype this information over and over again when visiting your favorite Web sites.

   ___

   Answers will vary

3. Where are cookies stored?

   Cookies are stored in Web browsers.

   ___

   Answers will vary

4. Certain free e-mail accounts use cookies to track Internet activity and personal information. Why are Web sites that offer free e-mail services not so free?

   Web sites offering free e-mail accounts aren't so free because you are providing personal information about your Internet activity in exchange for use of an e-mail account. These sites use cookies.

   ___

   Answers will vary

5. How can you protect your online safety?

   You can protect your online safety by controlling cookies, using strong passwords, installing and using antivirus software, recognizing and deleting suspicious e-mails, and restricting what you share on social media sites.

   ___

   Answers will vary

The R.E.E.L.

Directions: Read the scenario and answer the questions that follow.

What job scam red flags did Beth ignore?

The position is too good to be true. The salary is way above the range for the entry-level position that Beth has applied. Three days after Beth's interview, she receives a large check in the mail, unexpectedly. There are typos in the letter and the instructions direct Beth to deposit the check into her bank account and quickly wire a portion of the funds using Western Union.

NO LEGITIMATE COMPANY WILL EVER ASK YOU TO SEND MONEY TO THEM.

Answers will vary

Activity #1: The RIASEC Test

Answers will vary

Activity #2

Directions: Answer each question.

1. Write an elevator speech for yourself. Practice saying this speech with another person. How can you improve your elevator speech?
   Answers will vary

2. If a job recruiter were to Google your name, what three things would you like for him or her to learn about you? *Answers will vary*

3. Name two groups that you would join on Facebook? What does each group reveal about you? *Answers will vary*

4. Name two companies that you would follow on Twitter. Why would you follow each company? *Answers will vary*

Activity #3

Directions: Read each statement about taking courses online and decide whether you agree or disagree with it. Circle your answer.

1. A benefit of taking an online course is that you can take as long as you want to complete the course.

    Agree   (Disagree)

    Explanation: *This is an incorrect statement. Online courses are similar to classroom-based courses when it comes to completing assignments. There are deadlines and due dates for assigned reading and writing and participating in discussions.*

2. Online courses have the same rigor and expectations as face-to-face courses.

    (Agree)   Disagree

    Explanation: *This is a true statement. An online course will typically have a syllabus or course guide that outlines the reading materials, course schedule, learning objectives, assignments, and grading rubrics.*

3. You have support from many sources when you take an online class.

    (Agree)   Disagree

    Explanation: *This is a true statement. Typically, in addition to the professor, there is access to technical assistance, advising, and tutoring. Also, some programs have success coaches that will reach out to students who may be having difficulty and help them develop an action plan for successfully completing the course.*

4. If you enroll in an online course, you will be taught how to use a computer.

    Agree   (Disagree)

    Explanation: *When you enroll in an online course, you are expected to have basic computer and Internet skills. Some colleges provide* **webinars** *(i.e., meetings conducted over the Internet) and specialized training, but not knowing how to operate a computer effectively is not a valid excuse for not being able to complete coursework.*

5. Online courses demand engagement and a high level of involvement.

 **Agree**   Disagree

Explanation: *This is a true statement. The discussions in online courses require the exchange of ideas. Many courses require responding to discussion board questions, posting a personal introduction, and participating in group projects to foster learning and build community and presence.*

6. Most online classes require students to log-on only once during a given week.

Agree    **Disagree**

Explanation: *This is an incorrect statement. Most online classes require students to log-on several times a week to ensure active participation and maximum learning.*

7. Studies indicate students who succeed in online courses tend to procrastinate.

Agree    **Disagree**

Explanation: *Actually, studies indicate that students who succeed in online courses are self-motivated and independent learners. Such students have excellent time management skills and discipline and are able to complete assignments on time and meet deadlines.*

8. Employers do not accept online degrees.

Agree    **Disagree**

Explanation: *This statement is not true. Online programs must meet the same accreditation standards as residential programs that occur on campuses and in other traditional, face-to-face environments. Thus, employers do not distinguish degrees based on delivery mode. Furthermore, the ability to work in virtual teams is quickly becoming a required job skill, which is very advantageous for students who have the online course experience.*